God's Cheerleader

I0161266

LAUREY CARPENTER

DocUmeant *Publishing*
244 5th Avenue
Suite G-200
NY, NY 10001
646-233-4366
www.DocUmeantPublishing.com

Published by
DocUmeant Publishing
244 5th Avenue, Suite G-200
NY, NY 10001
646–233–4366

Limit of Liability and Disclaimer of Warranty: The publisher has used its best efforts in preparing this book and the information provided herein is provided "as is.

All Scripture quotations, unless otherwise indicated, are taken from the Holy Bible, New International Version®, NIV®. ©1973, 1978, 1984, 2011 by Biblica, Inc.™ Used by permission of Zondervan. All rights reserved worldwide. www.zondervan.com The "NIV" and "New International Version" are trademarks registered in the United States Patent and Trademark Office by Biblica, Inc.™

Scripture quotations marked "NKJV" are taken from The New King James Version / Thomas Nelson Publishers, Nashville : Thomas Nelson Publishers., Copyright 1982. Used by permission. All rights reserved.

Permission should be addressed in writing to:
publisher@DocUmeantPublishing.com

Edited by Anne C. Jacob, Popin Edits
https://AnneCJacob.com

Cover Design and layout by DocUmeant Designs
https://DocUmeantDesigns.com

Pompom Illustration 262205602 © Dmstudio | Dreamstime.com

Library of Congress Cataloging-in-Publication Data

Names: Carpenter, Laurey, author.
Title: God's cheerleader / Laurey Carpenter.
Description: NY, NY : DocUmeant Publishing, [2024] | Summary: "Two bits,
    four bits, six bits, a dollar, all for God's Cheerleaders, stand up and
    holler! Join Laurey Carpenter in exploring what it means to be a member
    of God's cheerleading team in today's society. Discover how ego,
    selfishness, greed, arrogance, and politics have overtaken pulpits
    around the world, and how we, the people, can work together to take back
    our church. Through thought-provoking stories, in-depth research,
    reflective questions, and inspiring quotes from the Bible, God's
    Cheerleader explains how: Man is killing the church Why Christians have
    a responsibility to ACT What is possible when we follow God's plan God's
    Cheerleader serves as a guide for individuals, families, prayer groups,
    and community organizations to identify and define their roles in
    society and to develop a strategy for bringing the world in alignment
    with the one that God has always intended for us"-- Provided by
    publisher.
Identifiers: LCCN 2024015911 | ISBN 9781957832364 (paperback)
Subjects: LCSH: Church renewal. | Church and the world.
Classification: LCC BV600.3 .C374 2024 | DDC 262.001/7--dc23/eng/20240607
LC record available at https://lccn.loc.gov/2024015911

To anyone who has been
hurt by the Church.
God has always been
present and loves you.

ACKNOWLEDGMENTS

To my dear friends, Charlene Trapp and Diana Curtis, for nudging me to find my voice and give me the courage to write and tell others to join God's cheerleading team.

I began writing, but fear kicked in and I started questioning myself. Much gratitude to Leah Miles and Kristi Tyrrell for building my self-esteem and cheering me on to complete the manuscript.

With my rebuilt self-esteem and courage, I started a Bible study and can introduce the first of God's Cheerleading team: Aimee Dickerhoff, Judi Eady, Julia Gennaro, Amy James, Leah Miles, Stephanie Mullins, and Kristi Tyrrell.

Contents

ACKNOWLEDGMENTS, V

INTRODUCTION, IX

PART I, 1

A Time to Keep and a Time to Throw Away

PART II , 23

Through Wisdom a House is Built

PART III, 35

Separation of Church and State

PART IV, 49

It's a Business: Let's Talk About the Money

PART V, 61

Service: Giving Back?

PART VI, 69

EGO vs. SOUL

PART VII, 77

The Seven Churches

PART VIII, 99

Call to Action

REFERENCE LIST, 107

MEET THE AUTHOR, 113

INTRODUCTION

FOR EVERYTHING, THERE *is a season*. Stunned, I sat up in bed. The early morning silence surrounded me as the voice in my head continued repeating the phrase, *for everything, there is a season*. Giving up on sleep, I went to my computer and placed those words into my Google search bar. When I read the truth, I broke down crying and shouted internally, AMEN!

For everything, there is a season, and a time for every matter under heaven:

> *a time to be born, and a time to die;*
>
> *a time to plant, and a time to pluck up what is planted;*
>
> *a time to kill, and a time to heal;*
>
> *a time to break down, and a time to build up;*
>
> *a time to weep, and a time to laugh;*
>
> *a time to mourn, and a time to dance;*
>
> *a time to throw away stones, and a time to gather stones together;*
>
> *a time to embrace, and a time to refrain from embracing;*
>
> *a time to seek, and a time to lose;*
>
> *a time to keep, and a time to throw away;*
>
> *a time to tear, and a time to sew;*
>
> *a time to keep silence, and a time to speak;*
>
> *a time to love, and a time to hate;*
>
> *a time for war, and a time for peace.*

(Eccl 3:1–8 New Revised Standard Version, Anglicised)

That morning in 2020, I awakened to two realizations, and when I acknowledged them in my mind and heart, a calming peace overtook me. The first was that preachers, elders, and people who are teaching the word of God are human, and they are my equals. Our Heavenly Father, God, and Lord, created each of us. He is the only one who needs to be placed higher. We are accountable to Him.

The second realization was that, in spite of my religious experiences, I am Bible illiterate. I know that I am an educated person. In my professional world, I am not afraid to ask questions or voice an opposing view. However, in my personal life, I have allowed and trusted *man* to speak and interpret the bible from the pulpit, and have taken each interpretation I heard as literal gospel. I need to learn the word of God for myself.

That was the day I decided to get a divorce. However, from the time I was a child, I was convinced that it was the gospel truth that marriages last forever. The fact that divorce is a sin had always been preached from the pulpit with enthusiastic religious fervor. Therefore, fear, ego, and the perception of what others would think overpowered me and kept me from taking action. I did not proceed until September 2021.

That was also the day that I realized the leaders of the church are human beings who are pressing their beliefs, opinions, and agendas upon the congregation. I was not serving God; I was serving man. I sadly realized that *Man is Killing our Church.*

It took me over fifteen years to get the courage to ask for a divorce. Southern traditions are still strong in the United States. Being raised in Florida, and then living in South Carolina for my whole married life, I think everyone can connect the dots and see why it took me so long to ask for a divorce. If not, I will explain it to you.

From the time I was a child, I was convinced that it was the gospel truth that marriages last forever. The fact that divorce is a sin was preached from the pulpit. I am a spiritual person and truly believe that God is protecting and guiding us. I believe that we all have Guardian Angels assisting us through our journey called life..

But guess what? Man is not the judge or jury for us. Our journey is our own. The individuals we encounter along the way will either be supporting us or trying to rob us of our happiness. The actions of others are not an excuse for the decisions each of us makes. At the end of your natural life, it will only be YOU and GOD. Judgment Day is yours and yours alone.

Part I

A Time to Keep and a Time to Throw Away

GOD AND ARCHANGEL Gabriel have been guiding me and pressing me to tell my story for many years. Throughout my adult life, and more importantly, starting at the time that I became a mother (1995), I became more aware of God's word being manipulated for man's personal gain. As my mother's instincts increased, my faith in the church was diminishing.

When I think back to my childhood, I realize that every moment was planned by God as he molded and guided me toward my adult life.

For as long as I can remember, I have been keenly aware that I was different. I would sit for hours and have long conversations with my imaginary friends. Together, we would hold wonderful teas and campfire chats. Many children have imaginary friends. Mine were different because they were real. I would always see them and loved play-ing with them every day. My mom would tell me to stop talking with myself. To this day, I believe these imaginary friends were and are my Guardian Angels.

Each human is covered in the love of Jesus Christ. He promoted a humble, honest faith in God, and used the innocence of a child as an example. Emulating the faith of children, we should simply take God at His Word. As children trust their earthly fathers, we should trust that our *"Father in heaven [will] give good gifts to those who ask him"* (Matt 7:11).

At the age of four, I was diagnosed with Child Absence Epilepsy (CAE). This is when a child will stare or become absent for periods of time. So, I went from imaginary friends to staring into space for periods of time. Yes! I was different. My mother ensured that I had friends who understood that I could not do normal things like others. Throughout my childhood, all I ever wanted to do was ride a bike, not be a rider, and swim underwater. These two things can be very dangerous for a child who spaces out at any given minute.

For as long as I can remember, my friend, *Shell*—I could not say *Michelle*—was there, and was my partner through-out my childhood. She would allow me to ride the bike, and she would be the rider. Until that fateful day when I drove us up a tree. All I remembered when waking up was Shell yelling at both our moms, "Why are you fussing on Laurey when I am the one that got thrown from the handlebars?"

This one childhood incident left a lasting impression on me for several reasons.

> **First**, *we all need to be able to expand our wings and fall on our own. This is how we grow. I can tell you that Shell would never let me ride the bike again. She learned her lesson in one bike accident.*

> **Second**, *although it was frightening waking up on the ground and not understanding what was happening, at least I can say I rode the bike. At least I tried. I had the courage to try.*

During elementary school, I would have to go to the school office to get my epilepsy medicine, so I was always the last one to go through the cafeteria line. Every day for six years, my friend Shell would wait for me at the doors of the cafeteria and go through the food line with me. Looking back, this remarkable act was done with probably no thought on her part. She was my friend, and that was what friends did. This is the beauty of the gift of love that we are given when we are born.

As a child, we instinctively comfort someone who is hurt or crying, or laugh when something is joyous. As we grow older, we tend to lose this childlike behavior. Well-meaning adults stifle our instincts. They tell us to "behave" or "act your age" or, better yet, "we're in public, behave yourself." As we grow older, there are unspoken "rules" to be rigid or presentable. Instinctive, childlike behavior is frowned upon, discouraged, or even considered rude.

As you can imagine, I had a *label* or a *stigma* to my name. I was *the* child who needed medicine to survive. Looking back, I am proud to have been *the* child. I had to learn at a young age that I am responsible for my own happiness and that having a few quality friendships was more important than having many friends. By the time I entered middle school, my CAE was gone.

Epilepsy is generational. Looking back, I realized my mother was protecting me and doing what she thought was best based on her experiences with the disease. Lessons are generational. Unintentionally, we learn from family members and accept their safeguards at face value. Sometimes, their guardianship can be harmful and isolate us from our loving Heavenly Father. My mother thought she was shielding me from harm and ensuring that I had a normal childhood, but epilepsy was not normal. Her protection was not malicious, but it kept me from learning about God. She loved me and wanted to ensure that I did not endure the pain she had experienced. I know she experienced more pain than joy growing up with Epilepsy. Her motherly instincts kicked in with me just as mine did with my children. This is my first

Funny side note:

One of my bridesmaids started dating our minister. My then-husband always said he didn't want details. I would reply, "he IS a man." Who knew that thirty-plus years later, I would write a book about him?

example of how man keeps us from learning about our soul's purpose.

Growing up, I was not a child who went to church every Sunday. I did not attend bible school or Vacation Bible School. My mother would always tell us we are protected, and that we are all God's children. Again, my mother was protecting me from having to go through what she experienced, which, in turn, stunted my growth in the Bible. When I did attend church, we would go to the local Presbyterian Church. For as long as I can remember, I have believed in God and that we are here to serve faithfully. When asked about which church I belonged to, I would state that I went to The Presbyterian Church or say that I was a Christian.

As a young adult, I started attending church regularly, and when I did marry, we had our Minister travel to my home-town and marry us at the First Presbyterian Church.

As a married couple, we attended church regularly and were actively involved members. I loved overseeing crafts for Vacation Bible School and teaching the two/three-year-old class on Sundays. I was enamored with the innocence of children and how they would soak up the stories and ask the simplest of questions that were challenging to answer. For example, why did God do this? I truly felt I was the teacher and the student at the same time, learning the passages simultaneously with the children. I would take note of their questions and find the answers later at home. Luckily, most children have a short attention span, and I was usually saved by a different question.

By 1999, we were a family of five. Busy is an understatement. We both wanted our children to have the background of attending church as a child. As we became more active in the church, our responsibilities increased, and we were asked to serve on additional committees. This is all good, however, when it comes to "church politics," the more we did for the church, the more popular we became in the church. Boy! Everyone thinks government political parties are a mess, but they haven't been a part of Church Politics.

I eventually realized that I was listening more to man and less to the written word of God. Life became a pattern of going through the motions. With our busy schedule, hearing the word of God from church leaders was easier and more convenient than learning the word of God for ourselves. I rationalized that the church leaders knew more than us about God's word. However, how did we know this was true? Although we attended church, we did not learn the word of God.

As any marriage goes, you have your ups and you have your downs. We hit a low point in 2006. I was hit with a trifecta of changes. Within a two-week period, I learned that my husband had accepted a job three counties over and we were moving. I found out that he was having an affair with a man. To add to the chaos, our daughter had an emergency appendectomy.

Okay! To say the least, that was a TRIFECTA. There was crying, yelling, and lots of cursing. I lost count of how many times I said "Why?". In life, you are always told you are never given more than you can handle. But DAMN! This was unbelievable. Where could I go from here? I was in a private, all-women's bible study at the time. What did I do? I said nothing. My pride would not allow it. My closest friends advised me to get a divorce. This was easy for them to say, because it was not their life. I married till death do us part. Funny, I advised some of my friends to get a divorce. It is easy to say, "Get a divorce," when you are not in the driver's seat of life.

My world was spinning, and I was grasping for control of my life. As everyone says, including me, you need to give control over to God. Or, as Carrie Underwood sings, "Jesus, take the wheel." Unfortunately, I handed the wheel over to man and not to Jesus.

We are all imperfect, but we strive to be perfect or correct in our decisions. It is painful to realize that there are no right or wrong decisions in life. The lesson is that you need to be at peace with your decisions. My decisions were focused on my children and my husband while I took a backseat in the car of life. I know this was when my voice became dim and was close to zero on the volume level. I know some women are reading this and are saying, "YES! I can so relate." It is not wrong or right, it is what we do. I call this the mom instinct. I became a robot with style. I wanted to portray a good life with successful children and a successful husband, and I was the driving force behind it. You know the adage, behind every successful husband, there is the woman. I was going to be that woman, damn it. I knew I had style and was willing to put myself on the back burner for those I loved. I put myself in the corner and chose to put my family above me.

Deep down inside me was a tug-of-war. My husband kept saying he wanted his family, but he had taken a job three counties away. I knew that whether we stayed together or not, the house needed to be sold. In 2006, I was working as a realtor, and it was a good real estate market. After the shock and crying fits, I sold our 5,000-square-foot, completely furnished house within three weeks. Trust me, I know why they say never make big decisions when you are in a crisis.

We found ourselves all crammed into a two-bedroom apartment that was only 1,000 sq ft. Right or wrong, I thought, I was doing this for the family. However, hindsight is 20/20. The anger finally set in, and in a moment of spite, I bought a house in my own name, in the same county as the apartment. I wanted stable housing for our children. I know that the neighbors in the apartment below us were thankful when we left.

As a wife and mother, I wanted to have a whole family and not be a statistic. As a Christian, men in the church had instilled in me that divorce was a sin. I was not about to give up when I hit a roadblock or a challenge. I loved my husband, and I married him through sickness and health till death do us part.

Determined to keep the marriage together, I insisted that we see a Christian counselor and that we do this together. Demanding a Christian counselor was honestly my first true encounter with man being in the cloak of Godliness. This is also where I began to develop my insight into men in the church pressing opinions, beliefs, and agendas on others through the guise of being Christian. My trust needed to be in God, not in man.

I need to back up a little bit and let you know that my husband wanted his family but was not too keen on couples therapy. However, when I added Christian couples therapy, he agreed because he wanted the family. I knew I needed God and thought the answer was a Christian Counselor. Again, I was naïve and turned to a human for my answers when the answer was truly to turn inward and be with God. Hey! Some lessons are hard to learn. Obviously, I needed more lessons.

We attended our first therapy session. I was under the impression that we were going to find out that we didn't communicate enough, or that we needed to carve out more couples' time and have date nights. Boy, was I mistaken. Issues arose from before we were married—talk about no communication. As a woman, I was blown away. My husband started with, "Laurey aborted my baby, and I was not given any voice in the matter." My head was spinning, and I was thinking, *it is 2006 and this occurred in 1991. Why is he just bringing this up now?*

I am a Christian, and I had an abortion. I believe we are born with our bodies, and we should have the right to decide what we do to our bodies. I am Pro-Choice. This will come up on

God offers us Mercy and Love. There is no reason to fear Judgment Day.

my day of Judgment; however, it is between me and God and no one else.

Now, back to the story. The Christian Counselor stated, "We need to stop couples therapy and we cannot proceed any further until Laurey attends an abortion grief counseling session."

I remember looking at him and saying, "What? I need to attend additional counseling?"

He reiterated that I had killed my child, and I needed to grieve and repent for my sins. In 1991, I had prayed, journaled, and grieved for my child-to-be. Now, because my husband stated that he had no voice in my decision, it was my responsibility to grieve again. At that time, my husband stated, "I will support you in whatever YOU decide." As a 23-year-old, I thought to myself, holy shit, I am in this by myself. He will support me, but I need to decide. This is not an easy answer. Mentally, I was in the Gone with the Wind scene where Prissy says, "I don't know nothin' 'bout birthing no babies.

OK! I hope you all have done the math. Fifteen years later, a Christian man is telling me I need to grieve again. I wanted my marriage to survive, so I went to Abortion Grief Counseling. I can say that I only attended three sessions. I am proud to say that I was part of the 40 percent that did not finish the program.

The ideology decreed during those sessions—of being a murderer and shunned in God's eyes—made me feel like

I was having an out-of-body experience. I knew that God loved me and only wanted the best for me. He made the ultimate sacrifice for me. So, for someone to tell me that I am frowned upon by God because I had an abortion seemed extremely wrong and ungodlike. Maybe that is why the sessions occurred in the basement of a church. The emotional trauma I received during those three one-hour sessions truly shut me down and scared me for years.

The Christian Counseling faded away, and we moved three counties over for my husband's new job. In retro-spect, the timing was Divine. When the real estate market tanked in 2007, I was able to find a new profession and have a clean slate. Since my husband was in Government Administration, I needed to find a profession that would be able to move with his job. My passion for community service became my career.

One's mind is a miraculous tool that can protect you from so many things. Therefore, it is no surprise that my Trifecta moment was pushed down and stored away in my mind for many years. I thought God had abandoned me and I was not one of the Chosen. I did grow up Presbyterian. We are the frozen chosen. I say 'frozen' because the Presbyterian church is rich in tradition. We stand when we need to stand, and we are quiet and speak only when spoken to. Too many times to count, my mother would say, "Remember Laurey, only speak when you are spoken to."

When I walked out of the abortion grief counseling group, I thought I had walked away from God and that God was glad that I was gone. But I didn't walk away, and God never gave up on me either. I turned inward and started studying the Bible on my own. I used a concordance and started studying verses from whatever word came to mind. This is where I learned that the word serve is in the Bible more than the word love. One day, I realized I had had the concordance before my trifecta moment. Then, I realized that God didn't leave me. He made sure that I had the materials to be able to still be with Him and be able to carry on my studies of Him.

The funny thing about life is that God ensures that you are on the right track or He will make sure that you get off that track to reassess priorities and be still centering yourself with the Divine. This happened to me on Mother's Day 2013. I was making banana pudding for my kids, and I tripped over the garage steps while taking the cans to the recycle bin. In an instant, I was headfirst planted on the garage floor with one ankle turned the wrong way (compound fracture) and a broken foot on the other. We were not aware of the broken foot on the other until post-op checkup ten days later. That might explain the falling when trying to hop on that foot to get to the bathroom.

This one mishap allowed me to be still (I had no choice) and look at my life and see if I was truly happy. I thought, overall, I am an optimistic person, but am I happy?

Full disclaimer, everyone's definition of happy is different. Take a moment and ponder your definition. Realize that at this time I had been in the nonprofit world for over seven years, and I took it even one step further. I thought nonprofits must have a mission statement and asked myself, *what is my mission statement*? So, in July 2013, my personal mission statement was ambitious, to say the least: Laurey Carpenter is a community leader who loves her family and community and leaves a lasting tangible impact to improve the lives where she lives.

Alright, go ahead. Do you think it is big? I look back on this and laugh. I see so much EGO in my mission statement. However, I put my words into action every time. I am happy, yes, happy to state that this mission statement propelled me and two dear Christian friends of mine to spearhead and build the largest ADA playground in an eleven-county region and to have our county named as an All-American City in 2018.

While I was still, I also realized that I needed therapy. I needed someone to talk to about my happiness and this feeling that I needed to find my voice. I was hesitant to find a Christian Counselor and thought maybe I needed to find a Life Coach. During this timeframe, that was the buzz—you need a Life Coach, not just a counselor. HAHA! I can say that I chose a counselor that used the buzzword Life Coach in his bio on the website.

I was in counseling on and off from 2015 through 2021. Over that timeframe, I had several ah-ha moments. One, I was having an affair with my community. I gave all my love and emotions to my county, an entity that cannot return the love and is nothing tangible; however, in turn, through my love and passion, I gave the county a new playground and a national title, something tangible. No wonder I was emotionally depleted and depressed.

A healthy relationship needs to be reciprocated. My husband and I poured our love into our community, but not into each other. My husband stated he wanted his family, but said nothing about marriage. We will always be a family. We have three beautiful, smart, and talented children. We will always be connected. I wanted a marriage. I loved my husband, but I was NOT in love with him.

Now, this is where the self-stress and self-doubt you place on yourself begins. Your little voice is filling you with negative feelings and self-inflicted stress. I learned that is my ego. Again, Divorce was a sin. That had been preached to me many times. I did not want to be a failure.

Who gave me the title of failure? Why wasn't I happy when I supposedly learned to be independent and find my own happiness when I was young? OMG!! I was on the hamster wheel, and I was repeating life lessons because I was not learning from them. I was not getting these nudges or being still long enough to truly listen to my heart. God woke me up in the early morning hours with the

statement, *everything has a season*. I had an emotional release; I started crying, and I knew that God was telling me that nothing is forever. There is a season for everything. The season of my marriage was over. This *knowing* gave me the courage to ask for separation and divorce. This gave me the courage to stay when he moved to the next county of his career.

When I lived in South Carolina, I would attend church. However, I can honestly say that after the Abortion Grief Counseling, I only attended occasionally. When we did attend church, we were introduced by my husband's title before our names. Again, this is man being in control of the Church. In addition, the times that I did attend, there was always a sermon on giving monetarily to the church. The giving was for improvements to the building, staff expenses, or capital campaigns to build a bigger church.

I am a woman with a serving heart. I know that we are on this Earth to make a positive difference and spread the love of God. Visiting churches where man was first, God was second, and money was the sermon became the norm, and I knew in my heart that this did not sit well with me. I know we are here to serve God and spread His love. Once again, serve is written in the Bible more than the word love. I love to serve. I love to make a difference wherever I live. I am walking on a path less traveled. I am comfortable with the decisions I have made, but what now?

When you venture into the unknown, it can be scary, but fun and exciting at the same time. I prayed and asked God, *what now*? I got this knowing or a feeling back, in the form of two great questions: What is your heart? What is your passion?

My first thought was, *what do I love to do?* I love to try new things. I am divorced with all my children grown. I have a clean slate and I am going to try new things. I am going to dive deeper into my spirituality. I think Church hasn't gone too well; I will try spiritual studies.

The church is the body of Christ—all the people who accept Christ's gift of salvation and follow Christ's teachings. It is much more than a building. In the Bible, "church" never refers to a building. It always refers to people—the people who follow Jesus Christ.

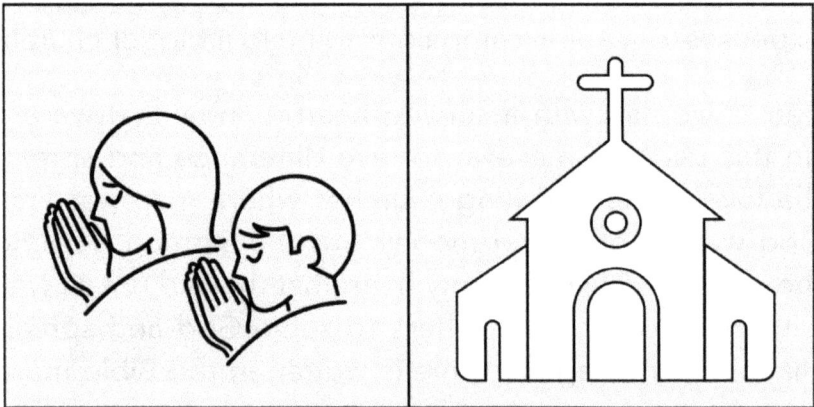

On my spiritual journey, I learned and embraced some wonderful practices. I know that this is controversial for some religious faiths, but I did several Reiki sessions. I found this to be soothing, and it brought clarity to me. I am happy to announce that I was visited by Archangel Gabriel and this session gave me the courage to write this book. Gabriel is God's Messenger.

Through attending a class called "Awakening your Ability," presented by Carol Cottrell (2022), and reading a book called MASTERING MANIFESTATION: *12 Keys to Unlock Your Hidden Potential and Live the Life of Your Dreams,* by Shannon MacDonald (2021), I have learned that regardless of what your beliefs are they are all similar and you need to follow your heart. AWW! One year into my adventures of spirituality, I realize that I am a CHRISTIAN and I believe that Jesus Christ is the son of God. He is my Savior and has a plan and purpose for my life. He wants me to live in abundance, peace, and love. He wants that for you, too!

WOW, really! Life is amazing. Lessons have different journeys. I feel that I have come full circle. I am a Christian and know I have lived these experiences to encourage others never to lose hope. I always ask what lesson I am learning. I know we are here to constantly learn and then teach others to improve the quality of life. Our God only wants the highest and best for all His followers. The lesson is that God is present and waiting for you to acknowledge His presence. He loves you.

For generations, slowly, the love of Christ has been silenced. The silence has occurred through man. Man has taught us that silence is golden. Actions speak louder than words. However, through silent actions, the praise of speaking the Holy truth and that God has been with us all along has fallen on deaf ears.

As I reflect, EGO (edging God out) is everywhere and man is diminishing the light of God, His source, and the belief in a higher being. We need to come back to our hearts and truly shine and do what is good for the soul, honoring Him as our Lord. Man is using the Church under the guise of religion and pushing their beliefs, opinions, and, in some cases, political agendas. Man is polarizing faiths and religions when we need to be coming together and working together for the welfare and well-being of each other regardless of our faith.

Over my lifetime, I have been a cheerleader in many different forms. I have cheered for sports teams, cheered for my husband's career, cheered for my children, cheered for my community, and cheered for myself internally. Who has cheered for God? I know that there are praise teams and worship teams. But who is God's cheerleader? Ah-ha! My heart belongs to Jesus Christ. I want to be God's Cheerleader. I am picking up my megaphone and shouting, "I love God, and God loves you!"

As I stated earlier, I am a servant. I have been hurt deeply, but my love for God has been constant. I silenced it. I am picking up my love for God and continuing to be a servant. I am self-nominating and self-appointing myself as God's Cheerleader. I am changing my paradigm and beginning to speak boldly about my love of God. I live in the freest country in the world, the United States of America. The Constitution's First Amendment gives us the right to speak freely and openly about our religion. I am bold, obedient, and follow my instincts. I am going to be God's Cheerleader.

Through my experiences, and my love for research, I have come across several topics that I am going to address, give some background, probe you to think about, and answer some reflection points. The topics are not warm and fuzzy; they're messy. These topics have stayed on my mind for the past few decades, and I know they need to come out into the light and be discussed in churches. Open and honest communication is one of the pillars of a strong relationship. The most important relationship is with God. Are you being honest with yourself, your family, your church family, and with God?

Reflections

Have you ever said the words, "Why God"? What was the experience?

Name some examples where God or your Guardian Angels have helped you.

Discuss a time when EGO hindered your thoughts or when your decision was based on your ego.

Deep down in your soul, what is your passion? Have you heard a calling that you want or need to pursue?

What do you need to keep in your life to follow your passion? What can you throw away that is keeping you from following your passion?

Part II

Through Wisdom a House is Built

EVERYTHING STARTS AT home. I know this is a broad statement, but it sums everything up. Children need the guidance of their guardian(s)/parent(s). Time and time again, there are examples of where the blame is on the school, the government, other people, or anyone except the primary parent or guardian. Accountability begins at home. Over the years, I have seen this word, *accountability,* pop up in levels of life. We are human and need to be held accountable for our actions. This could go either for the good or the bad. I am not here to discuss the merits of positive versus negative reinforcements. However, love, compassion, and understanding are traits that are best learned by example. A child needs these reinforcements everywhere, especially at home.

The Merriam-Webster Dictionary defines family as "the basic unit in society traditionally consisting of two parents rearing their children." Then, they add as an alternative definition for family, "any of various social units differing from but regarded as equivalent to the traditional family." This is where the home has differed, and man started altering the core definition of the family. Children need a loving home and guidance. They need family members to mold them to be sound and build a solid foundation for them physically, socially, and spiritually. A foundation is stronger with two pillars versus one pillar. If family members are in the community, the child or children will have a stronger foundation. I believe that a strong family starts with having two adults involved in the rearing, not just one.

According to the Annie Casey Foundation, in the United States today, nearly twenty-four million children live in single-parent families (Child Well-Being, 2023). This total, which has been rising for half a century, covers about one in every three kids across America. I am going out on a limb and stating that love, compassion, and understanding are not being seen by children on an ongoing basis. Children are consistently being shown anger, unlawfulness, and entitlement through video games, television, and lack of supervision. The family value of being raised by two loving parents has been diminishing since 1935. We also need to remember that this did not happen overnight. It has slowly grown louder and more relevant to the point that Americans are starting to recognize it and they are beginning to question what is happening.

We are all God's children, and we are all loved. As we grow, we become parents to a beautiful child, and this process repeats itself. As parents, we become teachers to our children. How we are taught today differs from how our parents were taught. These slight changes are ripples that can change the fabric of our thoughts and actions. I was astounded to learn that President Roosevelt stated that the continuation of the government relief program would be a bad thing for our country. Here we are. Almost 80 years later, the welfare system has grown to include over 80 programs, and over a trillion dollars was spent on these programs in 2022 (Biden's Budget, 2023).

The American government reinforced the new definition of family in 1935, with the new national welfare system, which was adopted under the leadership of President Roosevelt. I find it interesting that, according to the Teach Democracy website, in his State of the Union Address in January 1935, President Rosevelt "called for guaranteed benefits for poor single mothers and their children along with other dependent persons," and further into the speech, he argued and mentioned that a "continuation of government relief programs was a bad thing for the country," (National Welfare, 2024).

I've learned that if we stop growing spiritually, we start to die. Metaphorically, is your spiritual foundation solid? To grow spiritually, one needs to be grounded. The definition of grounded is to be well-balanced and sensible. A synonym for grounded is awake. People who are becoming grounded are awakening themselves and beginning to tap into

> **"All are called but few choose to listen."**
> **—A course in Miracles**

their intuition and listening with their hearts. For years, I was in a spiritual coma. I did not question, ask, or in some cases even defend the Lord's name, even when I knew what the people were saying was false. A phrase that I recently learned from an Evangelist on YouTube, Justin Peters, is that I am Bible Illiterate. I took everything at face value and did not take the time to read the scriptures and come to my own conclusions. Justin Peters Ministries is committed to communicating biblical truth through expository preaching and teaching resources designed to deepen the believer's knowledge of God and, in turn, his love for God.

Again, to grow in the word of God, you must start with a solid foundation. In today's world, there are more and more people who are mentally hurt and do not know how to get relief or understanding. In my therapy sessions, I was taught *Awareness, Choose, and Take*, or **ACT**.

> **Awareness**: *that something is off (or in my case, I am being Awakened to my Christian faith)*
>
> **Choose** *to change or take control*
>
> **Take** *action*

"The Lord by Wisdom founded the earth; By understanding He established the heavens; By his knowledge the depths were broken up, and clouds drop down the dew" (Prov 3:19-20).

Our heavenly father gave us tools to use throughout life. These tools are *wisdom* or insight, *understanding* which enables us to have good judgment or discernment, and *knowledge* or revelation.

My revelation is that in all aspects of life, Our God is speaking to us and providing the tools for us to make a good judgment that will increase our knowledge spiritually and on a personal level. To truly grow, we must learn or gain wisdom, make sound judgments, and grow with our knowledge to become the best person who we are meant to be. An average person would not be able to make this correlation unless they are awake and choose to take control or change and take action to become a better person.

Your future is dependent upon your foundation. When you are grounded, your foundation is strong, and you have the ability to use wisdom, understanding, and knowledge to make the conscious decision to become the person God intended you to be.

"Through wisdom a house is built, and by understanding it is established; By knowledge the rooms are filled with all precious and pleasant riches" (Prov 24:3-4 New King James Version).

As we grow, we must not be afraid to question someone's viewpoints or fact-check what they are saying. In the New Testament, we are continually warned of false prophets or false Gods. It is our responsibility to gain wisdom, make sound judgments, and use this knowledge to develop the courage to question policies and ideas that don't align with God's will. This can be difficult, especially when prominent individuals are publicly taking a stance or misrepresenting their beliefs for personal or financial gain.

Regardless of age, we are all children of God. We need to provide opportunities for children to be exposed to the love of God. This is hard to do when, throughout the generations, many of us have been hurt by individuals who are affiliated with a church. This happened to me. I was not part of a church family. When I did attend church, the experience of feeling welcomed was truly hit or miss.

This is not a new problem. It is written in the bible that there will be a time when man turns upon each other. This is happening in our churches today. We need to put our differences, egos, and man's agendas to the side, and make decisions that are from the heart, with God, Divine, our higher power, as the center when decisions are being made. That is why my time spent in the church has been few and far between, and I have resorted to studying the Bible myself.

I turned inward, went to a local Christian bookstore, and bought a Concordance of the Bible. Studying the Bible became looking up phrases I wanted to learn more about and reading the scriptures that coincided with the phrase of the day. I felt whole and complete with my individual bible studies. I felt grounded and bathed in the love of Jesus Christ. I also felt safe since no one was visually judging me like when I would visit a church.

Growing up, I was taught and told time and time again that if you cannot say anything nice, then it should not be spoken. I am not sure how old this adage is or who coined the phrase, but this is something that I have tried to live by throughout my life. Now, I am only human. I know at one time or another that you have heard something like this. Whenever I think of this phrase, I think of Jesus Christ saying you shall *"love your neighbor as yourself."* (Matt 22:39 NKJV)

I think this has been forgotten by many in the world. Take a moment and think about your words and actions in the last twenty-four hours. Are you happy and at peace with everything that you have done or said? I know many of us can think of at least one or two things that instantly come to mind. Whether you are at peace is between you and God. I am only here to bring awareness and remind you to show love according to how you want to be loved.

Love comes in many forms; it can be the love of a personal relationship, the love of a parent to a child, the love of a business partnership, or the love of serving your community. Regardless of what type of love we are talking about, respect is usually the underlying meaning in describing how or why love is mentioned in your description. The definition of love is an intense feeling of deep affection. The definition of respect is a feeling of deep admiration for someone, or something elicited by their abilities, qualities, or achievements. As you can tell, these words: love and respect, are very similar to one another, except that respect is more descriptive. Love is a simpler term and is used heavily throughout the Bible. In concordance, there are over three columns where love is

I have been told that most churches have an app and there are no longer church programs.)

mentioned. Love is synonymous with God. When I think of love, the first thing I think of is that God was the first person to love me and will be the last. I believe that God is the infinity of love.

The Bible has many verses that speak of love and the love for Jesus Christ, loving your neighbor. How can someone feel love when they attend a church service and they are ignored by the greeter at the front door or given the side eye look during the service when they sit where *that* person always sits, or the classic, you do not have the church service program and do not know the protocol of the service? A person has come to the church to be inspired and to hear the message of the Lord. They want to feel loved and welcome. Instead, it is an extremely awkward experience to walk into an unfamiliar church without first being introduced or knowing someone who regularly attends.

Change is a matter of life.

If you go on any social media app, you can see posts that give people thought-provoking stories to ponder. Such stories used to encourage kind and welcoming responses. I do not know when or how this simple act of kindness has degraded over the years. Online and in person, it seems as though outsiders are no longer welcome. If you are a member of a church, what are you doing to ensure that individuals feel welcome? Besides being a greeter, I call this person the one that hands the programs out. What do you do? Do you take the time to introduce yourself or have a committee that assists in the welcoming of visitors?

Reflections

Was there a time that you felt unwelcome? How did it make you feel? Did you ever go back?

Name one act of kindness that you have done and never mentioned to another person.

At your church, in what ways do you ensure (or what changes can you implement to ensure) that new visitors are welcomed and encouraged to become a part of the church family?

Over the next couple of days, write down every time you do something nice for someone and expect nothing in return. In what ways can you have this increase over time?

Now, in reverse, write and reflect on when someone has done some act of kindness to you. How did it make you

feel? Did it provoke you to pay it forward? If so, what did
you do?

Part III

Separation of Church and State

ACCORDING TO THE Library of Congress, our government, the American republic was founded on a set of beliefs that were tested during the Revolutionary War. Among them was the idea that all people are created equal, whether European, Native American, or African American, and these people have fundamental rights, such as liberty, free speech, freedom of religion, due process of law and freedom of assembly.

Liberty is the state of being free within society from oppressive restrictions imposed by authority on one's way of life, behavior, or political views.

Freedom of speech is a principle that supports the freedom of an individual or a community to articulate their opinions and ideas without fear of retaliation, censorship, or legal sanction.

Freedom of religion or *religious liberty* is a principle that supports the freedom of an individual or community, in public or private, to manifest religion or belief in teaching, practice, worship, and observance.

Due process of law is application by state of all legal rules and principles pertaining to the case, so all legal rights that are owed to the person are respected. Due process balances the power of the law of the land and protects the individual person from it. When a government harms a person without following the exact course of the law, this constitutes a due process violation, which offends the rule of law.

Freedom of assembly, sometimes used interchangeably with freedom of association, is the individual right or ability of people to come together and collectively express, promote, pursue, and defend their collective or shared ideas.

Our government was formed after the Bible was written. Our founding fathers wanted to ensure that all have the right to the freedom of religion. The First Amendment to the Constitution says that everyone in the United States has the right to practice his or her own religion, or no religion at all. I am blessed to live in a country where we have our freedom, and we can speak our own truth whatever that may be, and government, or the State, cannot interfere.

As the United States grew, the State evolved and established laws and protections to ensure that everyone has these freedoms, and in doing so, established protected groups. A protected group, protected class, or prohibited ground is a category by which people qualified for special protection by a law, policy, or similar authority. These decisions are made on Capitol Hill and through individuals that we elect to office. These elected officials are chosen by Americans that have the privilege to vote. This process is all from Man. We know that many views, opinions, and consensus through majority votes empower a few to identify with their geographical area and are supposed to represent the views of their service area. Like voting, being a representative for your constituents is a privilege and an honor. It is important to note that members of faith need to pray and/or meditate to give these officials the support and guidance to be a true representative of their elected service area. We live in a democracy; meaning, we need to respect the person who won the election even if we did not vote for them.

Today's society has many distractions. This is the intention of Satan. The more we are distracted, the farther away we get from the Holy Spirit and God's will. For generations, there have been 12 steps to assist with overcoming some type of addiction. I ran across the book, Walking the 12 Steps with Jesus Christ. This is sad, but true—all forms of addiction have elements of sociopathic behavior. In the book, sociopathic behavior is described as follows:

> A sociopath is a person who lacks social and moral responsibility. He knows that what he is doing is wrong but does not care in the least. He lives life only for himself and with total disregard for the presence of another. He is totally self-centered. He has extreme difficulty getting along

with others and at times does not even care to get along. It is always the other guy's fault in his social relationships. He sees no fault whatever in himself.

The sociopath loves to have no boundaries. "Don't fence me in with rules and Discipline!" is his motto. His value system is a momentary one that changes to suit his fancy, and his wants. He loves to lie and steal. He will often lie merely because lying is more fun to him. He is mischievous in his behavior because that gives him a "bang" inside. He cheats others even when it would be just as easy for him to get the same results by earning it.
(Geisel, 1996)

When I read these two paragraphs, my first thought was this is the United States Government. There have been so many scandals and immoral activities, with no account-ability, that you do not know what to believe. Depending on which news network they are watching, each average person is given a different narrative about what is hap-pening in our community, in our nation, or in the world. Remember, we are God's children, and we need to be cognitive that we are following the true God. There are so many idols and false gods that it is our responsibility to be discerning and review the information that is being given. We need to pause and truly meditate to see if what is being said is for the higher good of ourselves and for our Heavenly Father. This is not an easy feat. There are so many bad people that can look, sound, and have a moral and ethical façade, and when you look deeper, you only see sin and transgressions that go against all the things that our Lord wants for us, which are faith, hope and love.

"And now these three remain: faith, hope and love. But the greatest of these is love" (1 Cor 13:13).

Being a politician is hard, however, it seems that the individual in power spends most of their time getting re-elected instead of working for the people who placed them in office. Being elected should be an act of service in which you humbly serve the area that you represent. There are hard decisions that need to be made, and it is not a popularity contest. In the bible, we are called to serve and be faithful to the Lord.

"Each of you should use whatever gift you have received to serve others, as faithful stewards of God's grace in its various forms" (1 Pet 4:10).

As people searching for the Lord's message, we want to have inspiration, hope, and a mission to make our lives better or be of service to the community. When a person attends or visits a church, they are searching for other people that make them feel safe, welcome, and have kinship. God has spoken to them through their intuition or their heart and this person has taken the courage to step through their fear to come to your place of worship. In some cases, many days have gone by before they have enough courage to attend. A place of worship should be a sanctuary. ANY person should be welcome.

The world is becoming more polarized, and identity is being described in political views. Immigration, financial crises, abortion, and judicial rights are important and are being discussed in the political realm. But do these issues need to be discussed in a Sunday sermon from the pulpit? Man is erasing the separation of Church and State. Political views are being discussed from the pulpit. These are views of man, not of our Lord, Jesus Christ.

Should a Minister, Pastor, or the head of a church run for political office? I personally have known Ministers who have held local political offices. I believe that we are the steward of God's message, and we are here to share it first. Being in a political office makes it easier to push these polarizing views from the front of the church. Again, we are only human, and I pray every day that our leaders, whether political or religious, are given the wisdom to do what is best in God's name.

To genuinely hear God's message, you need to take the time to listen. I truly did not understand this until I had a compound fracture on the right ankle and a broken foot on the left. God made sure that I stopped. I know it was an accident; however, I know that everything happens for a reason. This idleness gave me an opportunity for reflection and to obtain skills that I am using today. I know that I would not have obtained these skills unless I slowed down and felt that I needed to be productive with my downtime.

My question is, are the leaders of the church taking the time to truly pray, listen, or meditate to deliver God's message? Throughout the years, I have witnessed a lot of discord, dissension, and unease within communities, nonprofits, and in churches. There is so much drama in the churches that there is no time to truly deliver with the word of God. The pulpit is used to calm the nerves of the rest of the congregation. It is amazing to me that one person or one family that has money, tradition, and legacy within the church can be more powerful than the actual Minister who is hired to lead the church.

Over the years, I have witnessed churches be divided when a new Minister begins. I would also like to add that this usually happens when you have a long-standing Minister preceding the new Minister. No one likes to change, however; that is how a person grows. Our God wants us to have an exceptional natural life. To truly experience this, you must grow. Change is a matter of life. For us to grow and have an exceptional life, we evolve, outgrow the present day, and move to learn a new lesson or experience something we never could have imagined.

I believe that many churches are stagnated, wanting to be "in control" and pressing Man's ideology onto the people instead of proclaiming the message of God. As I am writing this, the CBN network on Cable TV is running a segment on the Ethics & Religious Commission of the Southern Baptist Association. This segment is about how this commission works on Capitol Hill and uses its resources (money) to ensure that the beliefs of the Southern Baptist Association are represented and that the members of Capitol Hill are aware of their ideologies.

Man, members of this association, voted and agreed on their ideologies. This segment mentioned nothing about the first amendment and freedom of religion. I would like to point out that I only saw this one segment and I am sure there are examples where this commission is working on our freedom of religion choices. I truly believe it was Divine that I saw this segment before I sat down to continue writing this chapter on the separation of Church and State.

I would also like to point out that there are so many YouTube segments on how Generation Zs are moving away from the church or not even identifying with any religion. I can understand their mistrust and decision to move away from organized religion. It took me fifteen years to truly realize that I will still be loved by God after choosing to walk away from my marriage. I took my own walk with faith to understand that it is my journey, not the journey of the Church. Man has preached the sins of what will happen and not the joy or hope that comes with believing in God. For generations, from the pulpit, we have been told about the negative consequences of not being what man says about the bible. What about the joy—how God wants us to know what it is to love and be loved? For too many years, negativity and darkness have taken center stage. I am an upbeat person! Let the joy, light, and brightness of God be told!

Thinking back over my relationship with the Church, I was told how to think. Man impressed upon me what is good and what is bad for "our Church." The few times over the last seventeen years when I did attend church, political views were being compared to verses of the Bible, and used as reasons why we, the people, need to do something to protect our Church.

There are a lot of religious associations, committees, and organizations that are raising money to ensure that their religious and political views are being heard in Washington, DC. The Southern Baptist Association is only one example that I am giving since I saw it on television.

In 1936, the Government passed the Social Security Act, which established a system of old-age benefits for workers, benefits for victims of industrial accidents, unemployment insurance, and aid for dependent mothers and children, persons who are blind, and persons with disabilities. In my opinion, this is when the Government took the lead in assisting the needy and the Church took a backseat.

Fast forward to today, 40 Percent of all childbirths are out of wedlock. The government has made it easier for individuals to stay single and receive assistance. Remember that in 1935, President Roosevelt mentioned that this should not be a long-term solution for America. He stated,

> *"The lessons of history, confirmed by the evidence immediately before me, show conclusively that continued dependence upon relief induces a spiritual and moral disintegration fundamentally destructive to the national fiber. To dole out relief in this way is to administer a narcotic, a subtle destroyer of the human spirit,"* (National Welfare, 2024).

Through my professional experiences, I have witnessed where individuals have refused a promotion or a raise because their governmental assistance would be reduced. I have been told that they do not need an education, that they can just have another baby and receive additional monies from the government. We need to remember that this way of thinking did not happen overnight. This has been over 80 years in the making.

The growth of the birth rates to the growth of Supplemental Nutrition Assistance Program are similar. One should not be surprised, because when you have more children to feed, there is a greater need for food. This government program began in 1936 to assist the poor during the Great Depression, fast forward, and the demand is still there.

An interesting fact is people who make fewer than $20,000 per year are eight times more likely to contribute to their church.

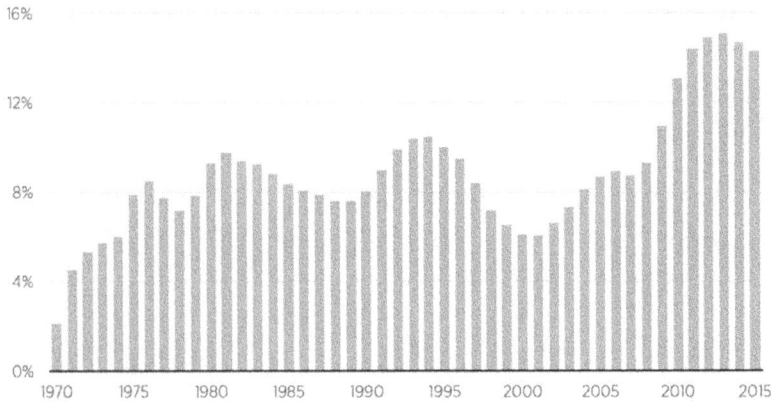

16%

12%

8%

4%

0%

1970   1975   1980   1985   1990   1995   2000   2005   2010   2015

MERCATUS CENTER
George Mason University

Source: US Department of Agriculture, Census Bureau.
Produced by Veronique de Rugy and Rizqi Rachmat, October 2016.

SNAP Participants as Percentage of Total Population (Rugy, 2016)

Biblically, Christians are instructed to help the poor. A great article titled "Is Welfare Scriptural?" was written in 2000 by Larry Burkett, in which he states:

> *No one can realistically deny the fact that the church is no longer the prime mover in meeting the needs of the poor; the government is. Nor can there be any doubt that from this base of government welfare, the "great society" has grown. From this society developed many families in permanent poverty, and because of this many Christians have developed resentment and indifference to the real poor.*

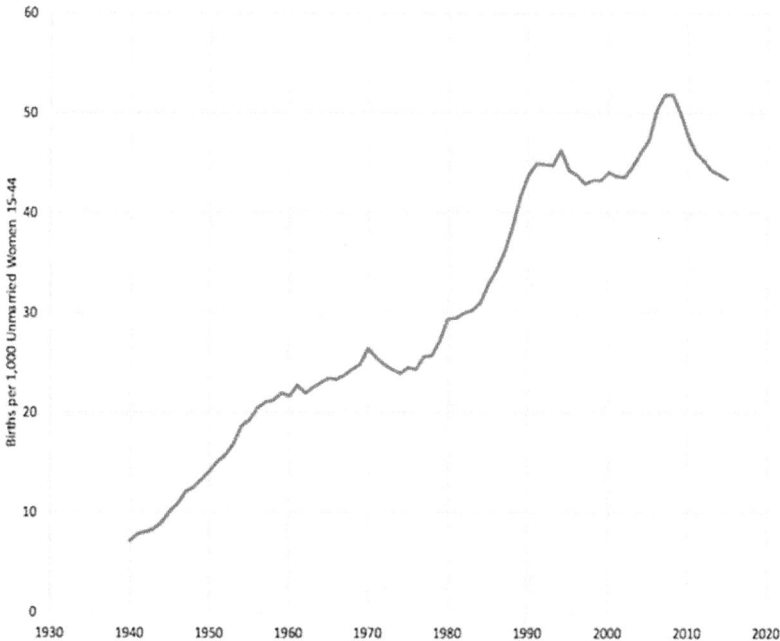

Source: Centers for Disease Control and Prevention, National Center for Health Statistics, various National Vital Statistics Reports. See the Source Notes at the end of the paper for more details.

Births to Single Mothers per 1,000 Single Women, 1940–2015 (VerBruggen, 2024)

I highly recommend everyone to look this up and read it. I concur that the Church needs to be more proactive in their communities and assist the needy.

Over time, the clear line between Church and State has blurred. The true calling of Christians to help those less fortunate is falling on deaf ears. Through the advancements of technology, increased access to news, and social media, the message of God is being diminished and being used for the gain of Man.

Reflections

How have you expressed your freedom of religion? Do you openly express it? Why or why not?

What are your thoughts on political issues in the church? What do you think about separation of church and state?

Have you discussed if a paying member of the church should be in a political office? Do you agree or disagree and why?

What are your thoughts on religious organizations having paid lobbyists on Capitol Hill?

Have you witnessed or noticed the diminishing of God's message? How?

Part IV

It's a Business: Let's Talk About the Money

FOR BASIC SURVIVAL, a human needs water, food, air, shelter, and sleep. All five of these elements are mentioned in the Bible. My belief is that the Bible is the Truth of God's teachings. This is what the Church needs to be focused on, and assisting to ensure that all who are without can survive.

An in-depth data analysis on monthly food costs appeared in an article on the website, BalanceEverything.com.

> *In the United States, the monthly cost of feeding one person is about $342.11. The average cost of food per day per person is $11.04. These are the insights provided by NUMBEO and their overview of food and other expenditures worldwide.* (Milena, 2023)

Now, let's talk about the money. The cost of feeding one person is $342.11 per month or $4,105.32 per year. To feed all Americans is $3.7 billion (331.9 million people times $11.04 per meal) per day. We know that not all Americans need assistance with food. For this example, I will take only the population described as poor. The official poverty rate in 2021 was 11.6 percent, with 37.9 million people in poverty. To feed the poor in America will cost $419 million per day or $152 billion annually (rounding up). The 2023 Federal Budget has a Supplemental Nutrition Assistance Program funded at $127 billion (Edwards, 2023).

An article written by Michael Singer on church revenue statistics includes a summary of where and how the money is donated to churches and religious institutions. Most donations are made by older adults, while young people in the United States rarely tithe. US Christians collectively earn $5.2 trillion per year, which is half of the world's total income. Less than 40 percent of Christians actually contribute to a church. An interesting fact is people who make fewer than $20,000 per year are eight times more likely to contribute to their church.

Some of the crucial church revenue statistics mentioned in Singer's article from EnterpriseAppsToday.com (2024) are as follows:

- ✦ Congregations in the US collect around $74.5 billion each year.
- ✦ Most donations in the US are given to religious organizations.
- ✦ US faith-based institutions account for combined yearly revenue of more than $378 billion per year.

- ✦ An average congregation records a yearly income of $242,910.
- ✦ The average weekly donation amount made per churchgoer is $17.
- ✦ Christianity is the wealthiest religion in the world.

With the above statistics, why are there still people hungry in the US?

Church is a big business. In the US, a church can be a non-profit organization. For tax purposes, churches are tax-exempt and do not need to pay any taxes on property and incoming donations. Also, as a religious organization, a church is not allowed to receive any federal funding. Again, faith-based organizations are not allowed to receive federal funding. The Small Business Association extended the Payroll Protection Plan (PPP) under the Coronavirus Aid Relief and Economic Security (CARES) Act to nonprofit groups, which normally wouldn't qualify through the agency. In all, the federal government gave more than $7 billion in loans to religious organizations. This was reported through ABC News in 2021. As a friendly reminder, these loans were forgiven if you pro-vided the proper paperwork.

How would I know this? As mentioned earlier, I have been part of the non-profit world for over fifteen years and am an accomplished grant writer. During the pandemic, I was part of a statewide non-profit that received PPP. When I was the CEO of a local Christ-like homeless shelter, I pro-vided the paperwork to ensure that the homeless shelter was approved for non-reimbursement. These loans were provided so businesses and nonprofits could remain open and continue providing services. At the homeless shelter where I was working, volunteers dwindled down to almost nothing. My question is, if churches received money to remain open, where were the church staff to ensure that our homeless were provided for? During this time and in my area, it was the businesses that provided the donations, monetary and non-monetary. Churches sporadically appeared and occasionally provided much-needed items and services to our residents.

According to an analysis by Religion News Service of data from the SBA, 13,408 religious groups, mainly churches, were approved for loans of $150,000 or more. Of those, 100 paid the loans back without asking for the loans to be forgiven. Fewer than 50 other groups were approved for the loans but did not withdraw the funds. In this same article, it stated that of those repaying their loans include loans that are being repaid, 99 Christian organizations and one mosque. Some were paying it back over time with interest. However, monies were given to non-profits. A Church is a non-profit. A lot of monies were given to organizations across America, including churches, for the Pandemic (Smietana, 2021).

When I think of a church, a nonprofit, or my community, my first question is, how can I be of service? With time, the first question in many minds when they think of these three entities is what can I receive? The United States has become the land of the taking. Churches and Christian organizations are saving their money or resources for a rainy day, better known as a rainy-day fund. On any given day, someone is in need. In Deuteronomy 15:11, the

Bible declares, *"There will always be poor people in the land."* The Bible also states, *"Whoever oppresses the poor shows contempt for their Maker, but whoever is kind to the needy honors God"* (Prov 14:31).

I have attended community meetings where leaders were asked, "what is one good thing that has happened to your organization through the Pandemic?" I witnessed leaders state that money was the best thing that has happened to their organization. As a leader, I stated that we were able to find permanent housing for four of our residents from the homeless shelter. In my words, you are a leader of a nonprofit to serve the community and provide services or improve the quality of life. Having money is a resource to provide the services. The money is a necessary tool, not a good thing that has occurred. What did your church or community do to increase the quality of life during the Pandemic?

By the end of 2021, volunteers began coming back and donations were increasing. At the Shelter, 85 percent of its funding is from donations. At the same time, the number of individuals who needed shelter increased, food costs skyrocketed, and overdue maintenance and equipment replacements put a strain on our organization. I found it interesting that church donations came in, however, not at the level that I was anticipating considering we were going through a Pandemic. We probably will never experience anything like that in our lifetime again.

Upon reading article after article, I have concluded that churches are pleasantly surprised and overwhelmed with the generosity of their congregations and the community at large. However, nonprofit organizations that truly serve the needy are at "ground zero" for providing the basic needs of survival: water, food, shelter, air, and sleep. In my community, I did not witness any increase in giving or donation of food or personal hygiene donations during the Pandemic. At a time of global crisis, I would think that more individuals would rally together to ensure that the community at large is being taken care of. Instead, I witnessed leaders posturing for being the lead organization and controlling the federal and state money that is being allocated for the county where I lived.

Churches come in all sizes, from small to mega. I think the term mega-church is like going through a drive-through and asking for the mega-size, please. By definition, a mega-church is a church that has a weekly attendance of over 2,000 people. Regardless of the size, tithing is part of Christianity. Tithe is a mathematical term meaning one-tenth, and is described in the Old Testament of the Bible. *"And all the tithe of the land, whether of the seed of the land or of the fruit of the tree, is the LORD's. It is holy to the LORD"* (Lev 27:30 NKJV).

As a woman of Faith, I believe that the book of Leviticus is about letting the life of the Holy Spirit bring you Faith and begin your growth in Godliness. This statement resonates with me because we are all here to serve, love, and help one another. It is written that it is our duty as man to give what we have to assist and "pay it forward" to others.

Man has turned the Church and the Faith of the individuals into a big business. Christianity is the wealthiest religion in the world. The word tithe has become a starting point for the churches. Man has made being a Christian a business. The government recognizes them as non-profits. As a nonprofit, you are supposed to have a balanced budget, meaning no net income. However, finance committees of any given church have the responsibility of ensuring they are solvent. Solvent could be taking your net income and making investments for the church. I pose this question to all church members: Do you know where the money is being spent? Is 10 percent of the church's earnings being spent in your community to serve, love, and provide hope?

Registered nonprofit organizations thrive on being transparent with their financial statements. It is required when asking for funds from large corporations. Nonprofits that are truly transparent have a location on their website where you can review their yearly financial statement. There are national databases where nonprofits upload their IRS 990, which is submitted yearly to the IRS. One database that I review is GuideStar.org. I searched for two churches in my local area and there was nothing reported. The reason I mention this is that if you are a registered nonprofit, I think the organization should fully disclose their financial statements. This includes churches. There should be nothing to hide.

Greed, one of God's greatest sins, is alive and well in America. There is even a television show called *American Greed*. This show exposes the downfall of individuals that have succumbed to greed and exposes the how, why, and where they are now. It is so popular that there are over fifteen seasons.

It saddens me when I see stories of a church inappropriately using their congregation's tithes. In February 2023, The Securities and Exchange Commission (SEC) of the government and the Church of Jesus Christ of Latter-Day Saints did separate press releases into the multi-year investigation of disclosure failures and misstated filings. The investigation covered the filings from 1997 to 2019. This resulted in a total of $5 million in penalties from the church and its investment management company, which is listed as a nonprofit too. This all occurred because a member of the church and an employee of the investment management company had the courage to come forward and become a whistleblower about the mismanagement of funds.

If you are a member of the church, do you know where the church money goes? Nonprofits should be fiscally sound and have accountability practices in place. We are all servants of God, and we have a responsibility to ensure that God's tool, the money, is spent in a fashion that is godly and that is servicing His higher power.

In Matthew 23:23, Jesus says, *"Woe to you, scribes and Pharisees, hypocrites! For you pay tithe of mint and anise and cumin, and have neglected the weightier of matters of the law: justice and mercy and faith. These you ought to have done, without leaving the others undone."* (NKJV)

It is you and only you that can answer this question. Are you tithing ten percent? *Tithe* in the Bible refers to ten percent of your annual earnings, productions, or possessions. One of your possessions is your skill set. There are more ways to tithe than through money. You could create and assist with the monthly newsletter or assist with the growth of the technical needs for streaming services online. Remember, tithing is to be seen as an accepted discipline, not as a law.

Reflections

How did your church provide for the needy during the pandemic? Are there areas that need improvements?

If your church received funds from the Payroll Protection Program (PPP) under the Coronavirus Aid Relief and Economic Security (CARES) act, what did it offer to your community to assist the needy? Did you pay back the funds?

Do you think churches need to be more transparent with their financials? Why or why not?

What skill set can you provide? Have you taken the time to see what special skills are in your church?

Do you feel it is a Christian's responsibility to help the poor? What can you do to help the poor? Do you want to help the poor?

Part V

Service: Giving Back?

OVER THE LAST five years, the weather has been very unpredictable and, in some cases, catastrophic. Living in the South, I pay attention to hurricanes more than blizzards. The Southeast has been hit very hard with damaging storms and major floods. Christians are the first to mobilize, raise money, and assist in any way that is possible. It is disheartening that you see the tsunami of service, love, and money only when there is a tragedy. Such acts should be everyday practices.

I love to serve. I started a volunteer-only nonprofit to improve the quality of life in my community. I had the passion, love, and underlying urge to serve and make the place where I live better. I have been silent while day in and day out, showing action of God's love and serving my community. An interesting fact, there are twice or maybe three times as many more verses where Love and Service are mentioned in the Bible than Tithe. However, when someone thinks of the Church, they say Tithe or give 10 percent to the church. I would like to flip it. Have you given 10 percent of your time to help your community be a better place to live?

Let's pause here for a moment and speak of transparency with the United States government. The United States Republic was founded on serving your congressional district and then have a regular paying career while not in session. Today, the average tenure of a congressman is 8.9 years. The longest serving congressman has over 45 years of experience. According to Quorum.com,

> The average age of members of Congress skews older than the average age of most Americans, with the average American being 20 years younger than their representative in Congress. As of 2015, 19 percent of Americans eligible to run for Congress are 65 or older. With Congress meant to reflect the diversity (including age) of the United States population, it's notable that 40 percent of current senators and 26 percent of representatives are 65 or older. Less than 5 percent of members of Congress are between the ages of 25 and 40, despite the fact that 33 percent of the over-25 population in the US are under 40 years of age. (Miller, 2022)

I bring this up to educate us on the makeup of the citizens that are making policies that run our country. Nonprofit organizations are intentional in the makeup of their board of directors, and they want it to mimic the demographics of their service area. This is not the case on Capitol Hill in Washington, DC. As the country grows, the demographics are changing and need to be represented when the country is making policy decisions. The only constant that needs to remain is on our founding principle, the freedoms of religion. There is a higher power and there are different faiths across our great nation, and I am proud to be an American and I am proud to be one of God's Cheerleaders. To Thrive, we the people need to ensure that we represent the demographics of the people that we are serving.

The purpose of the United States is expressed in the preamble to the Constitution:

> *We the People of the United States, in Order to form a more perfect Union, establish Justice, ensure domestic Tranquility, provide for the common defense, promote the general Welfare, and secure the Blessings of Liberty to ourselves and our Posterity, do ordain and establish this Constitution for the United States of America.*

More importantly, the country was founded on serving your congressional district. I am sure the service was not intended to be lifelong. Congress today has over thirteen members who have served for over 35 years (Miller, 2022). I know that there is a season for everything. How long is theirs? I question whether our statesmen are truly listening to God or if they are following a false god. Has man made serving for the betterment of the Country a personal gain? I say personal gain, since many of them increase their personal wealth while in the office. I find this interesting, since the salaries of Senators have remained constant since 2009.

As in Matthew 23:23, we have a responsibility to ensure that everyone has *"justice, mercy, and faith."* But how? We need to take the time to be still, reflect, and listen to our hearts. Everyone will have a different calling or specialty.

For some people, this is called prayer, meditation, or becoming one with self.

I want it noted that we are all children of God and we all are unique. That is the beauty of life. I ask everyone to take a moment and close their eyes and think: *I am loved, I am valued, and I am ME*. I can assure you that it will make you feel better. Although you are busy, take at least a minute each day to close your eyes and say, "Dear Lord, I know that I am loved, and I am here to serve you." Then be still and listen. Something will occur, or a thought will appear, or something will appear in your heart to take some kind of action.

I will give you an example. One of my best friends was diagnosed with an aggressive cancer. She is a *very* private person, and I am a *very* public person. I wanted to place her on every prayer list that I could think of. I was so distraught that I even thought about placing one of those posts about prayers needed on Facebook. I can say she would not be my friend if I did that. She is so private that she doesn't even have a Facebook account. I took a moment and prayed for her, and I instantly came up to send her a friendly short video every day. Yes! I did this for close to six months straight. I would do videos with some of the residents at the shelter, my children, or by myself. It was therapeutic for me, too. I was praying for what I could do.

This exercise was contagious and the small circle of just her and me became a little more. I am happy to report that she is in remission and getting her strength back. This one action helped so many people. It cost me nothing, not even time. I was doing what I do every day; however, I hit record on my iPhone, and for people who didn't know her, I would give her name and they would wish her well. Truly amazing, while doing your everyday task, you are sending a quick message to someone that you are being thought of.

Man is placed on Earth to serve; we are servants. The word servant(s) has over six pages in "Concordances to the Bible" on the "Bible Study Tools" website (2024). I can safely say that the good Lord wanted us to serve and help others through life. In addition, as a former executive of a nonprofit, I would like to say it is always great that you serve in a coordinated fashion. I am a big proponent of non-duplicated services. With all the people that are in America, you would think that everyone will have a bed, food, and love to have more than enough to survive. I understand that it is never as easy as I just wrote.

There are people who need help every day. My definition of help is going back to the five survival needs: water, food, air, shelter, and sleep. Are you aware of what is needed in your community? Do you know where to go to ask? Are you willing to donate some of your time to help these essential nonprofits in your community?

From Genesis all the way through to Revelations, there are many examples of being a servant and serving in the word of God. In the verse below, this is stating that God has kept his word and lifted the curse that was placed on Adam in Genesis 3:17. All good things happen to those that follow Him.

And there shall be no more curse, but the throne of God and of the Lamb shall be in it, and His servants shall serve Him. (Rev 22:3 NKJV)

Reflections

How do you serve God? What obstacles might sometimes keep you from serving Him?

When you hear the words *Serve* or *Servant*, what is the first thought that comes to mind? (I know this question can go everywhere; however, this is intended to bring your actions into a more Christ-like manner).

Do you know of any organizations that could use your help to serve your community? Have you stepped up, or how can you step up to help them?

How can you ensure our constitution and our freedoms remain? Have you ever taken our American freedoms for granted?

Do you know your neighbor's name and contact information? Do people in your neighborhood or surrounding neighbors look out for one another?

What can be done to assist the poor in your community?

Part VI

EGO vs. SOUL

THE EGO IS a person's sense of self-importance. Recognizing one's ego is a lifelong lesson and one that we will always be working on. Why? Because we are only human, and we will make mistakes. No one except God is perfect. In my class, Awakening Your Ability, I was introduced to this beautiful, well-written comparison of Ego versus Soul, Author Unknown.

There are so many examples above that we can talk about, but I am going to continue with my thoughts using realities from today, where man is consumed by ego.

When you turn on the television, many of the channels are sports, crime shows, news networks, and real-life reality shows. There is a new reality show called *Grown and Gospel*. From the one trailer that I saw, it is a lot of flair and shock tactics for ratings and money. The news networks keep harping on the investigations with the president's family and former presidents. I am witnessing opinions of man take center-stage, and in some cases, the law is being

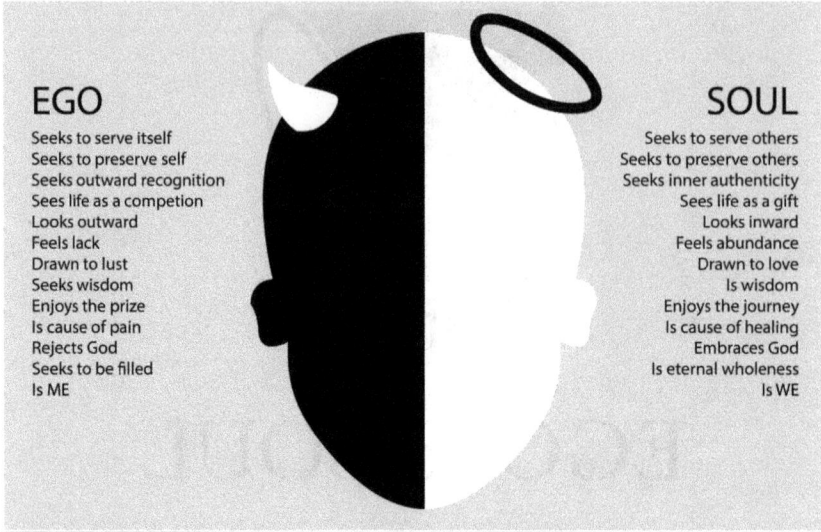

EGO

Seeks to serve itself
Seeks to preserve self
Seeks outward recognition
Sees life as a competion
Looks outward
Feels lack
Drawn to lust
Seeks wisdom
Enjoys the prize
Is cause of pain
Rejects God
Seeks to be filled
Is ME

SOUL

Seeks to serve others
Seeks to preserve others
Seeks inner authenticity
Sees life as a gift
Looks inward
Feels abundance
Drawn to love
Is wisdom
Enjoys the journey
Is cause of healing
Embraces God
Is eternal wholeness
Is WE

EGO vs. SOUL

ignored. For example, news outlets will only cover certain items to press their opinions on the people. This is being done regardless of your political affiliation. It is our own responsibility to do the research and see what is real and what is fiction.

You must have challenges in life to grow stronger. America is a young country; we are truly adolescents or even toddlers compared to other countries. The US was built on the freedom of religion. We must remember that, and be in the essence of we and not me. In addition, we need to become Bible-literate and speak up when we know that something is taken out of context.

Remember, my definition of *ego* is *edging God out*. Some pastors are making millions of dollars a year from the congregation's donations. If you do research, you can find lots of articles on how pastors have private planes, houses larger than most of their congregations, and lots of cars. But when a natural disaster occurs, these same Pastors do not open their church to those in need. When asked to explain why, they respond, "no one asked." This is disheartening, considering we are taught to love our neighbors and help in any way.

We have political leaders making deals to ensure they get votes to pass a bill. There is a whole profession in ensuring that man's agenda is heard, and it is called lobbying. Lobbying began in the 1600s, with the right of the people to speak freely with their elected representatives in the lobby of the chambers to voice their opinions. Now it is a formally regulated practice to advocate for organizations and businesses. This practice ensures that the voices of the organizations and businesses come before or in place of the voices of individual US citizens.

In 2022, $4.09 billion was spent on lobbying to our politicians who are responsible for establishing policies to ensure the wellbeing of the citizens of the United States. That is a lot of money to ensure that corporations can sway legislation for their betterment and not the betterment of the people. Another interesting fact is that Pharmaceutical and health product companies poured over a record $372 million into lobbying Congress and federal agencies, outspending every other industry and making up over half of all health sector lobbying efforts. Meanwhile, drug overdoses are astronomical. Opioid use disorder and opioid addiction remain at epidemic levels in the US. Three million US citizens have had or currently suffer from opioid use disorder (OUD). More than 500,000 in the United States are dependent on heroin.

I find it an interesting correlation that while the lobby numbers increase for the Pharmaceutical and health product companies that the number of people affected by opioid use disorder increases too (Sayki, 2022).

There are many enticements that are being placed in front of our elected officials. We need to pray that they choose soul over ego. As we know, we are only human, and ego is currently front and center. We need to ensure that the people of the US have the basic needs for survival. Coming full circle, it is the responsibility of the people to be accountable and ACT—be Aware, Choose to change, and Take action.

Over my tenure of working in nonprofit organizations, I have learned that people are scared. They have a scarce mindset. This mindset is generational. As a person of Faith, we need to spend time and communicate with our neighbors. Do you know your neighbor's name? Do you know the emergency contact information of your neighbors? It is our responsibility as man to increase the level of *faith* to everyone. The younger generations have only witnessed division and ego of man. When I say faith, I mean more than the love of God. According to Oxford Languages, Google's English Language Dictionary, *Faith* is "the complete trust or confidence in someone or something." The closest definition we get to the word *Faith* in the bible is *"Now faith is the substance of things hoped for, the evidence of things not seen."* (Heb 11:1 NKJV). Faith is eroding in America. Faith in our church leaders, faith in our justice system, faith in our political and community leaders. The divisive environment is everywhere. From local politics, riots and protests, business greed, and lack of separation of Church and State, where is God?

God has been here all along. I know this sounds so cheesy, but it is true. Man has us running, speeding, spending so much more time doing something for someone else that we are not listening. We need to stop, take a breath, and sincerely listen. If you are still, quiet, or spend time being with one, you will hear. I know this is scary. I didn't really want to listen. The entire world came to a stop for close to two years and I was awakened. Many are being awakened. That is why there are many changes. Man is starting to listen and there is a new normal. Have we taken time to listen to what man needs?

For me, I am pressed to write this book to stand firm and say that man is moving away from God's message. Do I have all the answers? No, but I am hoping this wakes more people up and begins the conversations of getting back to serving and spreading the love of Jesus' name.

Reflections

Which segment of Ego vs. Soul spoke to you the most? Why?

Share an example of a time that you witnessed more Ego than Soul in your life.

What are some ways you can change your actions to become more aligned with Soul?

Do you have faith? What do you truly believe without seeing and touching it?

Close your eyes and truly be still. What do you hear from your heart? What are you being called to do?

Part VII

The Seven Churches

I AM PROUD to say that I have been a cheerleader all my life. According to dictionary.com, the definition of a cheerleader is "a person who encourages and openly supports the success of a person or cause." Everyone has been a cheerleader at one time or another. You do not need to know how to do cheers, gymnastics, or tumbling to be a great cheerleader. We cheer ourselves on when we are facing fear, and we push ourselves through and accomplish the one thing we thought we could never do.

As mentioned earlier, fear is a part of our ego, edging God out. Our fear and pride sometimes have a louder voice, and we need to stop, recognize that we are listening to a false God, and start listening to the One and only Heavenly Father, Jesus Christ, and start cheering Him.

In the Bible, Jesus speaks of the seven different churches that will be in plain sight, and we need to make sure that we are listening through our souls and not through our egos. The seven churches are described in the Book of

Revelation, chapters 1–3. I realized that for the last fifteen years, I have been listening with my soul. I was living through the word of God and didn't even realize it. When I found this out, I sat on my bed, truly cried, and silently kept saying, "Hallelujah, Hallelujah!"

God's love is never-ending, and all these years, He has been protecting me and knew that I was not ready to be hurt again by man, and pressed upon me to have Faith, and pressed upon me to keep with his word. Regardless of how inadequate I felt, I kept leaning into the bible and His word. I am human, I am imperfect, and I keep working on myself and increasing my love for God, the One source that is never-ending and will be the only constant in my life. After reading over and over chapters 1–3 of the Book of Revelation, there have been so many times that I have encountered these different churches in my life that I felt inclined to give you my interpretation.

"I am the Alpha and the Omega," says the Lord God, "who is, and who was, and who is to come, the Almighty" (Rev 1:8).

"The mystery of the seven stars that you saw in my right hand and of the seven golden lampstands is this: The seven stars are the angels of the seven churches, and the seven lampstands are the seven churches" (Rev 1:20).

People are afraid of the unknown. When we read the book of Revelation, we realize that God has written the unknown and we do not need to be scared anymore. Our Lord is beautiful, and He has answered all our questions, and He does not want us to be scared anymore. Revelation is disclosure. What I love is transparency. All my adult life, I have strived to be transparent, and our Lord and Savior is nothing but transparent. If you are open, then nothing can hide or be hidden. It is hard to live this way, but you do not need to worry about what you have said or written. Today, we do not know what to believe or whether we can have faith in what is being said. There is so much discord, that now is the time to stand up and become God's loudest Cheerleader. Before we can be cheerleaders, we need to be awakened to the different types of churches that our Lord has forewarned us of, and we need to be living His word and being His light.

Church I: Ephesus

To the angel of the church in Ephesus write:

These are the words of him who holds the seven stars in his right hand and walks among the seven golden lampstands. I know your deeds, your hard work and your perseverance. I know that you cannot tolerate wicked people, that you have tested those who claim to be apostles but are not and have found them false. You have persevered and have endured hardships for my name and have not grown weary.

Yet I hold this against you: You have forsaken the love you had at first. Consider how far you have fallen! Repent and do the things you did at first. If you do not repent, I will come to you and remove your lampstand from its place. But you have this in your favor: You hate the practices of the Nicolaitans, which I also hate.

Whoever has ears, let them hear what the Spirit says to the churches. To the one who is victorious, I will give the right to eat from the tree of life, which is in the paradise of God (Rev 2:1–7).

Have you ever been to a church and have not felt loved? Many churches are quick to point the finger at you and state everything you are doing wrong. I would like you to point a finger at something right now. When you point a finger, have you noticed that your other fingers are pointing back at you? Always remember, when you point out one thing to someone else, there are three other fingers pointing back at what you need to correct yourself. Also, your thumb is more than likely lying on top of the three fingers. I call the thumb the silent nay-sayer that you are thinking about but not talking about. The church of Ephesus is a very important church to discuss. I truly feel that this is a church that is everywhere and so many have left their first love, which is the love of God.

When I was researching this church, I ran across a great article, "The Church and Ephesus," in which Rev. David Wilson Rogers states, *"Rather than uphold the sanctity of its Christian faith, the church had largely sold out to the political powers of the city. Rather than shine as a beacon of Christian faith, hope, and love. The church at Ephesus had aligned itself with the powers of darkness and embraced the vile nature of corrupt politics. For this, Christ warns the church in Revelation, that their prominence and blessing will be removed."*

This church embraces power and uses fear to rule. It does not promote love and service.

It saddens me to say, but I find it hard to believe everything that is said to us on television, radio, or when it comes to American politics. Many of our country's leaders are worshipping a false god and are only worried about themselves. As many know, for the last couple of years, there has been a border crisis in America. I would like to point out that neither Republicans nor Democrats are doing anything about it. Talk is cheap, and actions, more importantly, enforcing the laws of the land, should be a priority. The President of the United States has the authority to protect the people of the United States of America. We are not seeing it. Congress has the power to make policy to protect us; however, we have no policy, only another congressional committee to investigate something from the past and not being forward thinkers to protect the people that elected them to serve for their best interest. We are over $34 trillion in debt and there is always a 'false' showdown and then, mysteriously, an extension is made.

We the people are required to keep a budget and not allowed to overspend. However, we have a president who uses his executive action to provide billions for foreign aid to countries that are at war. The United States of America needs to protect its own border and love its people. The church of Ephesus can be used spiritually and politically. The United States of America was founded on the freedom of Religion and to allow all to pray to their Higher Source, which I call Jesus Christ. We need to open our

Bibles and spend time in the word of God. It is written. In addition, the USA needs to return to the basics and celebrate our Patriotic spirit at home. We need to demolish the political corruption, go back to what is written, and uphold our Constitution and our Bill of Rights.

The Church of Ephesus is a reminder that we need to return to being a person of light, love, and joy. It is simple: we need to put Christ first and center. It is our responsibility to make sure that we are being one with Christ, and He will lead us to Righteousness. Also, as Americans, we need to stand up and ensure that the law of the land is being followed by everyone.

Church II: Smyrna

To the angel of the church in Smyrna write:

These are the words of him who is the First and the Last, who died and came to life again. I know your afflictions and your poverty—yet you are rich! I know about the slander of those who say they are Jews and are not but are a synagogue of Satan. Do not be afraid of what you are about to suffer. I tell you; the devil will put some of you in prison to test you, and you will suffer persecution for ten days. Be faithful, even to the point of death, and I will give your life as your victor's crown.

Whoever has ears, let them hear what the Spirit says to the churches. The one who is victorious will not be hurt at all by the second death (Rev 2:8–11).

You might be suffering, and you might be materially poor; however, you are rich in spirit. Since the beginning of time, there has been suffering and many have been persecuted for their faith. Man has tried to change our beliefs; for example, Christians only celebrate Easter, which is only part of the resurrection of Christ. In the second century, churches in Rome began celebrating Easter as a replacement for Passover, which is one of God's annual festivals. Through the urging of uniformity of the churches, Pope Victor of Rome demanded that the Asian churches forsake the observation of Passover and begin observing Easter. This did not go over too well with the Asian churches, and they upheld, observing the fourteenth day of Passover according to the Gospel. I believe this is one of the first documented instances where man began deviating from the written word of the Bible.

The church of Smyrna is a reminder that being faithful to the word of God is hard. In some cases, you may be persecuted. We need to remember that Jesus held this burden and died on the cross, so we will be able to rejoice and celebrate his life and be able to be free of any spiritual burden. We are rich in the eyes of Jesus Christ. Persecution occurs every day. We hear of people who have been in prison for crimes that they never even committed. Around the world, you hear of people who have been beaten for having a different view or a different belief. For example, over the years, many journalists have been wrongly persecuted and placed in prison for spreading so-called misinformation. In America, we are fortunate to have freedom of speech. Many people take this for granted. I am now becoming a cheerleader. Being an American, I am blessed to be able to have freedom of Religion and freedom of Speech.

Church III: Pergamum

To the angel of the church in Pergamum write:

These are the words of him who has the sharp, double-edged sword. I know where you live—where Satan has his throne. Yet you remain true to my name. You did not renounce your faith in me, not even in the days of Antipas, my faithful witness, who was put to death in your city—where Satan lives.

Nevertheless, I have a few things against you: There are some among you who hold to the teaching of Balaam, who taught Balak to entice the Israelites to sin so that they ate food sacrificed to idols and committed sexual immorality. Likewise, you also have those who hold to the teaching of the Nicolaitans. Repent therefore! Otherwise, I will soon come to you and will fight against them with the sword of my mouth.

Whoever has ears, let them hear what the Spirit says to the churches. To the one who is victorious, I will give some of the hidden manna. I will also give that person a white stone with a new name written on it, known only to the one who receives it. (Rev 2:12-17)

How many times have you used the term, *double-edged*? I have a whole new appreciation of the term. I can safely say, I use this term more lightly than it was meaning. Here we are thousands of years later, and we are still encountering immoral actions without moral consequences. The Nicolaitans were a heretical sect of the church and strongly embraced false doctrines and thought that faith in Christ was a freedom from moral laws and repercussions. The closer we are to the people of the church, the harder it is to see the false doctrines, the human meaning of the word of God, and, more importantly, the corruption that is right in front of us. This brings another saying to mind: be careful of a wolf in sheep's clothing.

I am writing this to bring an awakening of seeing these false idols that are right in front of us, and to bring them out into the light. I want to shine a white light upon the darkness of sexual immorality and lying and praying to false gods and idols. I want to remind everyone of when President Clinton announced to America and the world that he did not have intercourse with an intern. During President Trump's civil and criminal trials, sexual misconduct was mentioned. Neither of these examples had a moral consequence for sexual immorality. We can fact-check politicians, news anchors, and pastors and find discrepancies. This is a warning for all of us to wake up. We need to be more astute and live in the truth of God's Word.

This is a wake-up call to all the people who are having sexual affairs, being immoral, breaking the law, or being deceitful; the good Lord knows and there will be retribution. Today, Satan is alive and thriving in America. Think of all the teachers, prophets, and pastors with similar corrupt influences. It is hard to notice; we need to strengthen our Lord's discernment in us and be ready to call a wolf a wolf and not mistake it for one of God's faithful sheep. One instance that comes to mind is the long-standing protection of pedophiles in the Catholic Church. This has been known for centuries and has been well known to be untouchable. Some Priests or high-standing leaders in the Catholic Church have been protected and have escaped accountability under the guise of statutory limits. Many have been suppressed and told not to talk about it. I truly believe this is why many, like me, have felt this and stayed away from the church. I am not Catholic; I am only using this as an example.

"For God, who said, 'Let light shine out of darkness,' made his light shine in our hearts to give us the light of the knowledge of God's glory displayed in the face of Christ" (2 Cor 4:6).

I would like to take this further and state that the Catholic Church has been lobbying in many states against the reform of the statute of limitations for sexual abuse. This is very important. According to stopabusecampaign.org, now that the secret is a well-known secret, the Catholic Church is trying harder than ever to stop these reforms. This removal of any limitations means the people of the church will not face any accountability for their sins. How can a person of Faith use God's name and the trust that children have in the leaders of the church, and hurt them to the human core, spiritually and physically? The statute of limitations for minor sexual abuse is when the victim turns eighteen years of age. For many victims, this comes to realization when they are much older than eighteen. It saddens me that this happens and there is no recourse for the victims to heal properly. We need to continue to pray for all who are involved. We do know that God knows, and it will be restored, and this immorality will be removed, and His righteousness will shine brighter than ever. Amen!

Church IV: Thyatira

To the angel of the church in Thyatira write:

These are the words of the Son of God, whose eyes are like blazing fire and whose feet are like burnished bronze. I know your deeds, your love and faith, your service and perseverance, and that you are now doing more than you did at first.

Nevertheless, I have this against you: You tolerate that woman Jezebel, who calls herself a prophet. By her teaching she misleads my servants into sexual immorality and the eating of food sacrificed to idols. I have given her time to repent of her immorality, but she is unwilling. So I will cast her on a bed of suffering, and I will make those who commit adultery with her suffer intensely, unless they repent of her ways. I will strike her children dead. Then all the churches will know that I am he who searches hearts and minds, and I will repay each of you according to your deeds.

Now I say to the rest of you in Thyatira, to you who do not hold to her teaching and have not learned Satan's so-called deep secrets, 'I will not impose any other burden on you, except to hold on to what you have until I come.'

To the one who is victorious and does my will to the end, I will give authority over the nations—that one 'will rule them with an iron scepter and will dash them to pieces like pottery'—just as I have received authority from my Father. I will also give that one the morning star. Whoever has ears, let them hear what the Spirit says to the churches (Rev 2:18-27).

Throughout time, the word Jezebel is related to a wicked, immoral woman. The bible states that she will consider herself a prophet. Today, being a single mother and having sex outside of marriage is common, and the United States of America normalized it when the New Deal was introduced by President Roosevelt and became law through Congress. This immorality has become a normal, everyday occurrence. As of 2021, the percentage of births to unmarried women has increased to 40-percent. The government has made it a beneficial and normal practice for couples to live in sin and stay unmarried to maintain their governmental benefits.

God knew that we were all imperfect, and he knew that this day would come when the moral value of the family would be deteriorated. How are today's children expected to learn moral and ethical values? We see it with the decline of the education system. There is no one at home to teach social etiquette, proper manners, and everyday expectations. This has moved into the school systems, and they are taking on the role of parenting from the parents. Children are allowed to change their birth gender without their guardian having a voice. This is being discussed on news outlets and will be decided in the court systems. I am purposely using guardian because a lot of the children have been born from children. My definition of children is anyone under the age of eighteen. How do you expect a child to raise a child? In these instances, the grandparents are stepping up and raising their grandchildren. Fundamentally, the definition of the family hierarchy is changing and allowing immoral acts to become normal.

Call me a prude or old-fashioned, I do not care. I truly believe every child's formative years should have a mother and a father. I raised my children to the best of my ability. They are self-sufficient and know that they are loved and will always have the support of both their mother and father. We are both only a call away. We both believed that our children needed a family to have the strong core values that they witnessed in both of us.

The Church of Thyatira is a testament to me that God hears us women and knows that females will be tempted, and he uses one of his seven Churches to acknowledge it. God speaks to us all, and we need to be open and listen. I cannot say this enough. Our moral fiber is always being tested, and this is a wake-up call to start heeding God's world. Remember, we are always being tested in one way or another; it is our decision alone whether to be tempted and go towards the darkness of Satan or to be righteous and go towards the light. In the world today, we need to be more discerning because our world is full of false gods, false prophets, and false promises.

Church V: Sardis

To the angel of the church in Sardis write:

These are the words of him who holds the seven spirits of God and the seven stars. I know your deeds; you have a reputation of being alive, but you are dead. Wake up! Strengthen what remains and is about to die, for I have found your deeds unfinished in the sight of my God. Remember, therefore, what you have received and heard; hold it fast, and repent. But if you do not wake up, I will come like a thief, and you will not know at what time I will come to you.

Yet you have a few people in Sardis who have not soiled their clothes. They will walk with me, dressed in white, for they are worthy. The one who is victorious will, like them, be dressed in white. I will never blot out the name of that person from the book of life, but will acknowledge that name before my Father and his angels. Whoever has ears, let them hear what the Spirit says to the churches (Rev 3:1-6).

I call this faking it till you make it. I grew up Presbyterian, and I always joked that we were the frozen chosen. Finding out about the seven different churches in the book of Revelation, Church of Sardis, reminds me of ME. I would go through the motions, take my children to church, sit on the "correct" bench in church, and go through the motions, and truly did not understand the meaning behind any of it. I was a "good" Christian. After reading these verses over again, I realized I was truly spiritually dead. I was not ALIVE in the word of God.

I am putting on my cheerleading uniform and standing up and shouting through my megaphone. Stop! Wake-up! It is great that you are going through the motions and practicing your faith. We need to stop practicing and start feeding our faith. How do we feed our Faith? It is easy. Make time and go to a Bible study, pray, and more importantly, have fellowship with other like-minded people who want to dig deeper into the love of God. It was pressed upon me, and I took the initiative to learn with others. I put fear aside and started a bible study. I reached out to one of my friends and we are a group of 5-6 woman who are coming together in fellowship and learning the Bible together. It is that simple. I tend to make things harder for myself. I had to move through the fire of fear and make that initial phone call to a friend, and state that I was "thinking" of wanting to attend a bible study. Today, we are five women who love Jesus and are yearning for the Holy Bible. I know it is so much easier said than done. Please! If a 55-year-old divorced mother can do it with no other knowledge; then I know you can do it. Again, I am raising my megaphone and cheering you on!

Church VI: Philadelphia

To the angel of the church in Philadelphia write:

These are the words of him who is holy and true, who holds the key of David. What he opens no one can shut, and what he shuts no one can open. I know your deeds. See, I have placed before you an open door that no one can shut. I know that you have little strength, yet you have kept my word and have not denied my name. I will make those who are of the synagogue of Satan, who claim to be Jews though they are not, but are liars—I will make them come and fall down at your feet and acknowledge that I have loved you. Since you have kept my command to endure patiently, I will also keep you from the hour of trial that is going to come on the whole world to test the inhabitants of the earth.

I am coming soon. Hold on to what you have, so that no one will take your crown. The one who is victorious I will make a pillar in the temple of my God. Never again will they leave it. I will write on them the name of my God and the name of the city of my God, the new Jerusalem, which is coming down out of heaven from my God; and I will also write on them my new name. Whoever has ears, let them hear what the Spirit says to the churches (Rev 3:7–13).

Do you know the story of The Tortoise and The Hare? The moral of the story is that being the fastest doesn't always win the race. However, this story can be an example of the Church of Philadelphia for me. The hare can be Satan and mock the true believers of God, the tortoise. The Tortoise is slow and steady; He is consistent in his Faith. As believers, we need to be consistent in the Word of God. The Hare has a condescending attitude and thinks he can win regardless, even if he lays down and takes a nap. Satan's people think they will always win. However, regardless of how fast you run towards the throne of heaven, you will not finish before the true believers of God.

It is hard for us to remain faithful Christians when there are so many hostile and adverse evil environments that we must endure. Although we are weak, and our Faith might be faltering, it is important to remember that we are still being faithful. God has issues with the "haters" of the church. We, as Christians, are being rewarded for patiently enduring His Word despite our strength in Him being weakened. This speaks volumes to me. God never gave up on me when I was lost and trying to survive in the world while raising my children and keeping our family together.

God woke me up and said, "there is a season!" I sincerely believe, from the bottom of my heart, I am here to become your cheerleader captain and provide you with the encouragement that you are weak, but you are not forgotten. God is here, and he wants you to know that he is going to keep you from the hour of trial for being faithful, even during your weakened state.

Church VII: Laodicea

To the angel of the church in Laodicea write:

These are the words of the Amen, the faithful and true witness, the ruler of God's creation. I know your deeds, that you are neither cold nor hot. I wish you were either one or the other! So, because you are lukewarm—neither hot nor cold—I am about to spit you out of my mouth. You say, "I am rich; I have acquired wealth and do not need a thing." But you do not realize that you are wretched, pitiful, poor, blind and naked. I counsel you to buy from me gold refined in the fire, so you can become rich; and white clothes to wear, so you can cover your shameful nakedness; and salve to put on your eyes, so you can see.

Those whom I love I rebuke and discipline. So be earnest and repent. Here I am! I stand at the door and knock. If anyone hears my voice and opens the door, I will come in and eat with that person, and they with me.

To the one who is victorious, I will give the right to sit with me on my throne, just as I was victorious and sat down with my Father on his throne. Whoever has ears, let them hear what the Spirit says to the churches (Rev 3:14-22).

Let me ask again, does your church give back to their community? Is there full transparency of finances? There are many people that are monetarily wealthy and do not need or want anything, because they have everything. But do they? Jesus is most upset with this church. You are lukewarm. You are content and are selfish for only thinking of yourself.

We are on this great planet to show the love of God, serve others, and remain Faithful in His word. God gave you riches, so you can spread his love further. In my years of working in the nonprofit world, I have witnessed this lukewarm more times than not. We need to be passionate and excited about the word of God. The Bible states that we are to tithe. Are you or is your church giving a tenth of your riches to spread the word of God and serve those in need in your community? Are you being an example that others want to emulate?

I have been silent for so long that I am picking up my cheerleading megaphone and shouting to all that can hear or read (laughingly) that I am a child of God and I know that I am loved. I know that I am being put in a place to encourage others to become a part of God's Cheerleading team. It is not a time to be silent or lukewarm.

Reflections

Re-read the verses from the Book of Revelation for each of the seven churches. In your own words, write a word or phrase to describe each church.

I. Ephesus

....

....

....

....

....

II. Smyrna

....

....

....

....

....

III. Pergamum

....

....

....

....

....

IV. Thyatira

....

....

....

....

....

V. Sardis

....

....

....

....

....

VI. Philadelphia

....

....

....

....

....

....

....

VII. Laodicea

....

....

....

....

....

....

....

....

....

....

Which of the seven churches descriptions most interested you? What did you find intriguing about it?

How can you use examples from the seven churches to help someone or yourself to get through a difficult situation?

Part VIII

Call to Action

THE REPUBLIC, THE United States of America, was founded on freedom of religion and freedom of liberties. However, over the last seventy-plus years, our government has taken a lead role in providing for the humanity of USA citizens. In Matthew, we are reminded that it is our responsibility to care for all people.

Then the righteous will answer Him, saying, "Lord, when did we see You hungry and feed You, or thirsty and give You drink? When did we see You a stranger and take You in, or naked and clothe You? Or when did we see You sick, or in prison, and come to You?" And the King will answer and say to them, "Assuredly, I say to you, inasmuch as you did it to one of the least of these My brethren, you did it to Me" (Matt 25:37–40 NKJV).

As Christians, we have a responsibility to provide for the poor. However, the government has enabled the poor to stay poor. I have witnessed individuals trying to get out of poverty, who are faced with the blessing of obtaining a raise from their employment, but accepting the raise will hinder their governmental supplements. When someone faces this test of faith, most of them choose the path well worn and stay on the government supplements. God is always testing us to see if we, as Christians, will step out in faith and choose the path less taken.

Yes, Faith is about being true to yourself. Ten years ago, I would not have believed if someone told me I would write a book about Faith and following in God's path and being true to self. We are on this Earth only once, and it is our responsibility to live life to the fullest. It is also our responsibility to serve others and to live the life that God has intended for us all along. We need to pray, be still and listen to God, and have the courage to speak the truth. This is part of the action that all of us are here to do.

Below are potential action items that you, your church, or your community can review and discuss to help improve the quality of life where you live:

1. Be aware of how your community responds to needs. What is the poverty rate where you live? What are the most needed items for their proper survival? What are your local churches or religious organizations doing?

It is Man's duty to ensure that we are all surviving. There will always be someone thriving, surviving, and barely making it. Collectively, more can be accomplished. Personally, I have always approached projects using the trinity method; one-third by government, one-third by the people, and one-third by businesses, foundations, and/or organizations. I have already disclosed that, monetarily, the government is the leader and the main player in assisting the poor. This is breaking the foundation of the United States of America.

Change begins with being aware of the problem. I am writing this book to bring awareness to this problem. I ask that individuals and leaders of communities, churches, and government leaders come together with solutions to assist the poor. I am not asking the Government to fund everything. I am asking the local churches, individuals, and organizations to come together to serve in unity and without duplicated services.

When I say that man is killing the church, perhaps I should say that man's actions and inactions are killing the church. Ego, selfishness, greed, arrogance, and politics have overtaken pulpits around the world. We, the people, need to take back our church. We need to be the church.

2. Be proactive in having more transparency in the church. Churches are nonprofits; they need to start acting like one. Be the catalyst to have more transparency with the financials and the revenues of the congregation. I challenge all churches in the United States to put forth 10 percent of their gross revenues towards the needs of the poor. Why are people starving and homeless when churches collect billions of dollars every year? Where is that money going? It is our "responsibility" as Christians to assist and help serve to the poor. Remember, there will always be those in need. God will always provide for his people; hence, why do churches have investment groups for a "rainy day"?

It is our duty to question and ask the hard questions. We do not need to follow blindly what the leaders of the church are saying. We need to make sure that we are following the Godly message and not following false gods. Prosperity is given to those that are obedient to God's word. God's word is written in the Bible. What is God is speaking to you when you are in prayer or sitting silently and trying to listen to God? This is easier said than done. I truly understand. There are a lot of noisy individuals and groups that say they are God's messenger; heck, I am even saying it in this book.

What is pressed upon me is to say is that it is okay to question something if it does not feel right in your soul. I know that for years, I have silently questioned what was preached to me; however, I never asked the messenger. I am empowering everyone who is reading this to ask the question. I can assure you that you are not the only one who is wondering what the answer will be. Have you been in a meeting, and someone asks a question, then several others jump in and ask other questions related to the same material, and they usually start their question, "Good Question. I was going to ask…"?

This is how change begins, and it is messy, but we need to go back to the basics and use all our resources for helping the poor and not to hold on for paid leaders of the church to prosper. Remember, everyone prospers when you help the poor.

My rule of thumb as a leader of a nonprofit is to try to keep administrative costs down to 15 percent of an annual budget, where 85 percent of the budget goes to program services for nonprofit organizations. Have you looked at a church budget the same way? Churches are nonprofits and they get all the benefits of a nonprofit. Why do they not follow the ethical practices of nonprofit organizations?

I am reminded of the lyrics to the 1972 children's worship song turned popular hymn, "We are Church," by Richard Kinsey Avery and Donald Marsh. *"The church is not a building; the church is not a steeple. The church is not a resting place, the church is a people."*

3. Identify your passion, and volunteer. Are you giving back to your community? Are you being a servant of God? There is always a need for volunteers. Have you given any of your time to a worthwhile organization or volunteered at an organization that shares the same passions as you? God wants us to serve. I challenge every one of you to give at least four hours a week to one of your passions. Your passion could be walking dogs at the nearby shelter or starting a YouTube channel about something that you are passionate about that the world needs to hear. Unexpected blessings occur when you are doing something that you are passionate about.

4. Maintain a soul perspective. Take a moment and review the Ego Vs. Soul picture. Review and journal on all the differences. I know that I have been on both sides of the spectrum for every one of these. It is important that we keep this front and center when making everyday decisions. It is easy to have a narrow perception of issues. I am encouraging everyone to look more holistically and have a soul perspective more times than an ego perspective.

5. Be God's Cheerleader! I have always been a cheerleader. There is something empowering to me about cheering a team to victory, cheering a loved one throughout their life and celebrating milestones, or more importantly, cheering God's messages to the world. In today's world, there are so many messages coming at you that you do not know what to take as fact or fiction. I have spent more time fact-checking the fact-checking, since the internet and social media have diminished people's trust. I am here to tell you that there is one message that has never changed: God's message. Now, there have been many interpretations of God's message; this is where only you can do the fact-checking and listen to your inner voice on what sounds right or wrong.

I am self-nominating, and self-designating myself as God's Cheerleading Captain. Do you want to join my team? There are no tryouts, no routine you must memorize or learn. The only thing you need to do is listen and act on God's word. It is time that all of humanity stop, listen, and act in a Christ-like manner and stop Edging God Out in your everyday way of life.

It is not the responsibility of the Government to feed the poor; it is all the Christians in America. With religion being one of the wealthiest industries, doesn't it make you wonder why the poor are growing in numbers and not decreasing? We the people were given freedom of religion when the United States was formed. This freedom or right was extremely important to our founding fathers; however, America has lost its way and trust in the American Government. God is testing us—and we as Christians need to follow His path.

It is time to stand up, cheer for all the Christians in America, and start action groups in communities across America. Make a difference in your community. We have the resources; we need to leave our egos at the door and truly sit down, have hard discussions about what is needed, and volunteer to do our part. This is not the time to sit back and point fingers across the table. The church needs to ACT. We are the church. We need to take responsibility and ACT.

Be Aware. Choose to change. Take action.

Two bits, four bits, Six bits, a dollar, all for God's Cheerleaders, stand up and Holler!

Cheers to you and the difference you will make in the world!

REFERENCE LIST

Azadfard, Mohammadreza, Huecker, and Leaming. "Opiod Addiction." National Library of Medicine, National Center for Biotechnology Information, 2023. https://www.ncbi.nlm.nih.gov/books/NBK448203/#:~:text=Three%20million%20US%20citizens%20and,in%20a%20year%20time%20period.

"Bible Concordances." Bible Study Tools, 2024. https://www.biblestudytools.com/concordances/.

"Biden's Budget: A Future that's Built on Government Dependence." Budget Committee, 2023. https://budget.house.gov/press-release/7582#:~:text=In%20fiscal%20year%202022%2C%20the,%249%2C000%20spent%20per%20American%20household.

Burkett, Larry. "Is Welfare Scriptural?" Crosswalk.com, 2000. https://www.crosswalk.com/family/finances/is-welfare-scriptural-507392.html.

"Catholic Church Had a 'Playbook for Concealing the Truth'." Stop Abuse Campaign, 2022. https://stopabusecampaign.org/protect-children-from-child-sex-abuse/roman-catholic-church-protects-priests-abuse-children/.

"Child Well-Being in Single-Parent Families." The Annie Casey Foundation, 2023. https://www.aecf.org/blog/child-well-being-in-single-parent-families#:~:text=In%20the%20United%20States%20today,every%20three%20kids%20across%20America.

"Church Issues Statement on SEC Settlement." The Church of Jesus Christ of Latter-Day Saints, 2023. https://newsroom.churchofjesuschrist.org/article/church-issues-statement-on-sec-settlement.

Cottrell, Carol. "Awaken Your Ability" Workshop attended 2022. https://carolcottrell.com/.

"Creating the United States Founded on a Set of Beliefs." Library of Congress, n.d. https://www.loc.gov/exhibits/creating-the-united-states/founded-on-a-set-of-beliefs.html.

Edwards, Chris. "SNAP Spending Doubles to $127 Billion." CATO Institute, 2023. https://www.cato.org/blog/snap-spending-doubles-127-billion.

Geisel, Ray. *Walking the 12 Steps with Jesus Christ.* Ocala, FL. Christian 12 Step Ministry, Inc. 1996. https://www.christian12step.org/.

"The History of the Debt." Treasury Direct, n.d. https://www.treasurydirect.gov/government/historical-debt-outstanding/#:~:text=(In%20

1835%2C%20the%20%2417.9%20million,bearing%20debt%20was%20paid%20off.

McDonald, Shannon. *Mastering Manifestation: 12 Keys to Unlock Your Hidden Potential and Live the Life of Your Dreams.* n.p. Divinity Speaks, LLC, 2001.

Milena. "Average Food Cost per Month—In-Depth Analysis and Trends." Balancing Everything, 2023. https://balancingeverything.com/average-food-cost-per-month/#:~:text=In%20the%20United%20States%2C%20the,for%201%20person%20is%20%2479.08.

Miller, Claire. "Who are the Longest Serving Members of Congress?" Quorum, 2022. https://www.quorum.us/data-driven-insights/who-are-the-longest-serving-members-of-congress/.

"A National Welfare System." Teach Democracy, 2024. https://teachdemocracy.org/bill-of-rights-in-action/bria-14-3-a-how-welfare-began-in-the-united-states.html#:~:text=Although%20President%20Franklin%20D.,first%20time%20in%20American%20history.

Oben, Patrick. "What Was the Doctrine of the Nicolaitans?" Patrick Oben Ministries, 2024. https://patrickoben.com/doctrine-nicolaitans/.

"Our American Government." 2023, H. Con. Res. 139, 108th Congress. https://www.govinfo.gov/content/pkg/CDOC-108hdoc94/pdf/CDOC-108hdoc94.pdf.

Peters, Justin. "Preaching God's Word Around the Globe." n.d. https://justinpeters.org/.

Rogers, David W. "The Church and Ephesus." Current Argus, 2018. https://www.curren-targus.com/story/life/faith/2018/01/27/church-and-ephesus/1066333001/.

Ryssdal, Kai and Leeson. "What Would it Take to Balance the Federal Budget?" Marketplace, 2023. https://www.marketplace.org/2023/02/08/what-would-it-take-balance-federal-budget/

Rugy, Veronique de. "The Historical Rise in Food Stamp Dependency and Cost." Mercatus Center George Mason University, 2016. https://www.mercatus.org/research/data-visualizations/historical-rise-food-stamp-dependency-and-cost.

Sayki, Inci. "Despite Record Federal Lobbying Spending, the Pharmaceutical and Health Product Industry Lost their Biggest Legislative Bet in 2022." Washington, DC. Open Secrets, 2023. https://www.opensecrets.org/news/2023/02/despite-record-federal-lobbying-spend-ing-the-pharmaceutical-and-health-product-in-dustry-lost-their-biggest-legislative-bet-in-2022/

"Senate Salaries (1789 to Present)." United States
        Senate, n.d. https://www.senate.gov/senators/
        SenateSalariesSince1789.htm.

Singer, Michael. "Church Revenue Statistics 2024 The
        Growth of this Religious Charitable Institution."
        EnterpriseAppsToday, 2024. https://www.enterpri-
        seappstoday.com/stats/church-revenue-statistics.
        html#google_vignette.

Schwartz-Lavares, A., Abubeyu, and Yamdada. "The
        Inequities of PPP: Megachurches, Large
        Corporations Receive Money Ahead of Small
        Businesses." ABC News, 2021. https://abcnews.
        go.com/US/inequities-ppp-megachurch-
        es-large-corporations-receive-money-ahead/
        story?id=75331197.

"SEC Charges The Church of Jesus Christ of Latter-day
        Saints and Its Investment Management Company
        for Disclosure Failures and Misstated Filings."
        US Securities and Exchange Commission, 2023.
        https://www.sec.gov/news/press-release/2023-35.

Smietana, Bob. "For Some Churches, Paying Back
        PPP Loans is Better than Forgiveness." Religion
        News Services, 2021. https://religionnews.
        com/2021/11/02/for-some-churches-paying-back-
        ppp-loans-is-better-than-forgiveness/.

"Total Lobbying Spending in the United States
        from 1998 to 2022." Statista, 2024. https://

www.statista.com/statistics/257337/
total-lobbying-spending-in-the-us/

Treybig, David. "Smyrna." Life Hope & Truth, 2024.
https://lifehopeandtruth.com/prophecy/
revelation/seven-churches-of-revelation/smyrna/.

VerBruggen, Robert. "How We Ended Up With 40
Percent of Children Born Out of Wedlock."
Institute for Family Studies, 2024. https://ifstudies.
org/blog/how-we-ended-up-with-40-percent-of-
children-born-out-of-wedlock.

"What is the Church?" Questions about God and Faith,
Faithward (website). Reformed Church Press,
n.d. https://www.faithward.org/what-is-the-
church/#:~:text=In%20the%20Bible%2C%20
%E2%80%9Cchurch%E2%80%9D,more%20
and%20more%20like%20Christ.

Yang, Jenny. "Percentage of Birth to Unmarried
Women in the US 1980-2021." Statista, 2023.
https://www.statista.com/statistics/276025/
us-percentage-of-births-to-unmarried-wom-
en/#:~:text=This%20statistic%20depicts%20
the%20percentage,has%20increased%20to%20
40%20percent.

MEET THE AUTHOR

LAUREY CARPENTER GREW up in Central Florida, where her mother's giving nature and her father's optimistic spirit led her to follow her passion for helping those in need. She raised three children, earned a bachelor's degree from the University of Florida, obtained her real estate license, became a grant writer, and volunteered in various community organizations, including as a CEO at a homeless shelter.

After years of working to improve her community, Laurey realized that Man was slowly killing the church—so slowly that few people were aware of it. She noticed that un-Christlike actions and policies had become accepted practices in multiple religious and community organizations. This realization compelled her to take action and provide a conversational starting point for putting mankind back on the road toward love and well-being.

Laurey is now the self-appointed captain of God's cheerleading team, passionate about helping others improve their lives and dedicated to spreading God's love, light, and blessings throughout her community and the world.

In writing God's Cheerleader, Laurey hopes to awaken others and give them the awareness and encouragement they need to start following their true Father of Heaven.

To join God's Cheerleading team

visit www.LaureyCarpenter.com
and sign-up for Laurey's monthly newsletters.

Together, we can spread God's love and help
teach love and blessings to all.

Follow Laurey on Social Media